Rising Expectations

Polis Center Series on Religion and Urban Culture
*David J. Bodenhamer and Arthur E. Farnsley II, editors*

*The Polis Center Series on Religion and Urban Culture aims to make the ideas emerging from innovative projects on religion in American cities available to a wide audience. Individual volumes will focus on specific cities, but each will ultimately seek to interpret national or global concerns as they are played out in real-life settings. By viewing broad social issues through the lens of local experience, we hope to illuminate the changing relationship between religion and contemporary urban culture in ways that are useful not only for scholars, but also for policy makers, clergy, social service and health care professionals, and the many others who deal daily with religion in its urban context.*

ARTHUR E. FARNSLEY II

# Rising Expectations

## Urban Congregations, Welfare Reform, and Civic Life

INDIANA
University Press
Bloomington & Indianapolis

This book is a publication of

Indiana University Press
601 North Morton Street
Bloomington, IN 47404-3797 USA

http://iupress.indiana.edu

*Telephone orders*   800-842-6796
*Fax orders*   812-855-7931
*Orders by e-mail*   iuporder@indiana.edu

© 2003 by Arthur E. Farnsley II

The paper used in this publication meets the minimum requirements of American National Standard for Information Sciences—Permanence of Paper for Printed Library Materials, ANSI Z39.48-1984.

Manufactured in the United States of America

**Library of Congress Cataloging-in-Publication Data**

Farnsley, Arthur Emery.
   Rising expectations : urban congregations, welfare reform, and civic life / Arthur E. Farnsley II.
      p.   cm. — (Polis Center series on religion and urban culture)
Includes bibliographical references and index.
   ISBN 0-253-34195-7 (cloth : alk. paper)
   1. Church and social problems—United States. 2. Church charities—United States. 3. City churches—United States. 4. Community organization—United States. I. Title. II. Series.
   HN39.U6 F37 2003
   261.8′3—dc21

                                                                                    2002010628

1 2 3 4 5   08 07 06 05 04 03

# Contents

# Preface

As many of the figures and statistics in this book are drawn from the research of The Polis Center at IUPUI's Project on Religion and Urban Culture (PRUC), a brief word about the project is in order. The PRUC was a multifaceted attempt to engage the people of Indianapolis in a conversation about religion's public role. It contained a research component, but it also comprised public literary festivals, collections of creative writing and photography, consultation with dozens of civic groups, nine books, two video series, and more than 80 research notes and newsletters. It also included public presentations in a variety of communities, from high school classrooms to neighborhood associations to the mayor's office. More information about PRUC products is available at www.thepoliscenter.iupui.edu. Information about the most recent video series—*Faith and Community: The Public Role of Religion*—is available at www.faithandcommunity.org. All of the PRUC products are meant to stimulate conversation among nonspecialist audiences about religion's role in public life.

The PRUC used both historical and sociological research methods in an effort to understand the relationship between religion and community life in seventeen Indianapolis neighborhoods, selected to represent the many sides of the city. These neighborhoods ranged from inner-city to "in-town" to outer suburbs. From 1996 to 1999, student researchers were provided training in the use of detailed census forms and sent to local congregations to retrieve relevant data. Numbers in this book about congregational membership size, percentage of members who live in the neighborhood, budgets, and mission spending are self-reported by representatives of the congregations, usually the pastor. A total of 413 congregations completed census forms, representing well over 75 percent of the congregations in the neighborhoods studied.

The purpose of this data collection was to allow comparison of congregations and neighborhoods in the city for purposes of research as well as civic discussion. The methods were experimental. Although graduate students managed the neighborhood research teams, college students did much of the data collection on the appropriate forms. In one instance, a high school class—under the supervision of their teacher—collected data in their local neighborhood, going so far as to create a videotape of their experience studying religion and community. Relevant data was presented publicly in each neighborhood and the comparisons discussed at city-wide events.

As part of the ongoing effort to be a public resource, between 1997 and 1999 I served as a proposal referee and adviser to programs such as the Front Porch Alliance, Juvenile Court, the Coalition for Homelessness Intervention and Prevention, Community Development Block Grants, and others. In each case, I was invited to serve as a volunteer community "expert" and not as a paid consultant or evaluator. I received permission to analyze the grant applications I read; to honor that trust, no applicants or other participants in the review process are identified here unless they received a grant as a matter of public record. My observation of those many efforts in their early stages helped me to assess their rationale and to describe the congregational participation in them. Any evaluation of their eventual success or failure will have to be the subject of a different book.

The datasets collected by the PRUC are housed in an Access database at The Polis Center at IUPUI. That database was analyzed using the NUD*IST tool for qualitative analysis and SPSS for relevant quantitative variables. Further information, including access to the data and a list of SPSS variables, is available at www.thepoliscenter.iupui.edu. Much of the data presented in this book has been published previously—sometimes using earlier data iterations—in various editions of *Research Notes from the Project on Religion and Urban Culture,* also available from The Polis Center.

The surveys referred to in the text were conducted traditionally. One is a 1997 survey of 600 inner-city residents, 150 in each of four selected neighborhoods. The second is a 1999 city-wide survey of 806 respondents on questions of religion and community life. A third is a 2000 survey of 260 Indianapolis clergy members. All were conducted by the Indiana University Center for Survey Research. The statistics from the US Census and those about grant applicants are self-explanatory and have been published elsewhere, as cited.

# Acknowledgments

The Polis Center Series on Religion and Urban Culture, including this inaugural volume, stems from the Project on Religion and Urban Culture. Authors always say that many people deserve credit for their work, but so many have contributed to the Polis Center and to the project that it is impossible to thank all of them as they deserve without making the acknowledgments longer than the book.

Thanks first to the Lilly Endowment for their generous support. The Project on Religion and Urban Culture took shape in the mind of the Endowment's James Wind, now president of the Alban Institute, and David Bodenhamer, director of the Polis Center and of the project. The Endowment's vice president for religion, Craig Dykstra, later became our program officer. I hope the books in this series will repay in some small way both Craig's guidance and the Endowment's trust.

Over the course of six years, more than a hundred people worked with the Project on Religion and Urban Culture as researchers, administrators, public teachers, writers, and clerical staff. I cannot list them all, but I am especially indebted to a few colleagues: Kevin Armstrong, Monty Hulse, Elfriede Wedam, Etan Diamond, Mary Mapes, David Licht, Karen Feitl, Michelle Hale, Jason Skelton, Robert Cole, Susan McKee, Dawn Parks, Alexis Simmons, Tommy Faris, Cynthia Cunningham, John Neal, and Jim Stout. Kevin has read the manuscript in drafts and guided me through the last year of work. Thanks, man.

A few other colleagues in the academy have been especially helpful: Jay Demerath, Jan Shipps, Bill Mirola, Pat Wittberg, Sheila Suess Kennedy, and Bob Wineburg. I also need to thank some advisers from outside the academy, people who read what I wrote and led me to believe, sometimes contrary to the evidence, that my time and effort might be worthwhile: John Hay, Bill Stanczykiewicz, Judith Cebula, Tim Streett, and Julanne Sausser. I apologize to any others who deserve to be on the list.

I need to thank many editors, including Edward Queen, who included an essay of mine in the volume *Serving Those in Need: A Handbook for Managing Faith-based Service Organizations* (Jossey-Bass, 2000). Thanks to Steve Smith at *Non-Profit and Voluntary Sector Quarterly,* Darren Sherkat at *Review of Religious Research,* and David Heim at *The Christian Century* for publishing my articles on this topic. Thanks also to Sage Publications and the Religious Research Association for permission to cite from those articles at length here. I am grateful for the guidance of the late Sarah Polster of Jossey-Bass. She saw an earlier version of this manuscript, and although she decided it wasn't right for Jossey-Bass, she was a great help to me in tightening it up. Thanks to Amy Sherman for commenting on a draft of my booklet, *10 Good Questions about Faith-based Partnerships and Welfare Reform,* in which I framed many of the issues addressed here. And, of course, thanks to Peter-John Leone, Bob Sloan, Jane Lyle, and Elizabeth Yoder at Indiana University Press for taking on the series and making my manuscript much better than it would have been.

As I have not won an Academy Award, it sounds like a cliché to thank my wife, Gail, for "making all this possible." But I said exactly that in my first book, and it is truer now than then. I wrote this book because I think the issues in it matter, but I need to thank my daughters, Sarah and Caleigh, for helping me remember that some things matter more.

Sincere thanks to the Indianapolis pioneers in faith-based partnership whose activities appear on these pages. To then-Mayor Stephen Goldsmith, Deputy Mayor John Hall, and Bill Stanczykiewicz (again); to Judge James Payne and M. B. Lippold at Juvenile Court; to Dan Shepley, Stephanie Lowe-Sagebiel, and other folks at CHIP: thank you. I hope I was some help when I was reading proposals and trying to share what I knew about the local religious scene. Although this book emphasizes my considered judgment that great caution is required in faith-based reforms, I have never doubted that each of you, in your own considered judgment, was trying to make the world a better place.

Thanks, finally, to my mother, Linda Berger, a committed Christian who has headed a local economic development office and directed a nonprofit educational program for youth, and who now serves as an elected official. I still remember going door to door at age seven, distributing little jack-o-lantern door hangers that read "Even the Great Pumpkin is Voting Nixon-Agnew" because Mom was a precinct committeewoman. So I think she gets some of the blame for the fact that this book, like my first book, *Southern Baptist Politics* (Penn State Press, 1994), mixes two of the three subjects that it is impolite to discuss over dinner. Finally, my mother was also my last copy editor for *10 Good Questions.* So thanks, Mom. This is for you.

Rising Expectations

# 1  Introduction: Congregations as Community Organizations

> Most Americans are now well aware of the devastating chain of circumstances that has undermined once robust inner-city communities over the past two decades. . . . But this essay is not about pessimism. Quite the contrary, it is about the remarkable hope being rekindled in communities across America. Faith communities are at the center of this good work. . . . When I say faith communities I mean churches, mosques, temples—religious institutions of all faiths. Religious institutions have a unique potential to contribute to community rebuilding. (Cisneros 1996)

Religious congregations—churches, synagogues, mosques, and temples—have recently been called upon to play a much larger role in the creation and maintenance of civic life. The administration of George Bush Sr. aimed to energize America's "thousand points of light." During the Clinton administration, the government turned more directly toward partnerships with the private sector, especially with congregations. The unique role of faith-based groups became a foundational tenet of the George W. Bush administration.

Civic leaders of all kinds deem congregations capable of a variety of tasks, from improving the delivery of social welfare services to rebuilding a sense of local community that many fear is missing from our lives. There has been a vibrant debate about public funding, about the kinds of restrictions that should or should not be imposed, and about constitutional issues. But the assumption that congregations can and should do more in our public lives goes nearly unchallenged.

The problems for which congregations are sometimes proposed as solutions are very real. Many Americans do feel disconnected from the broader community. They have only a weak sense, if they have any at all, of participation in civic life. They are plagued by either the reality or the specter of violent crime linked to pockets of serious poverty.

There is a pervasive feeling that many of the institutions that have attempted to shape and maintain our common public lives are incapable of doing so. We are disengaged from the political process, as evidenced by consistently low participation in elections. Although many people say that the government should fix the problems of crime and poverty, few are confident that it can. Many feel alienated from the marketplace—some because they feel subjugated and manipulated, but others because they have abandoned the notion of vocation.

Many of us change jobs and careers numerous times throughout our lives. Public schools, especially in big cities, are often perceived as weak and ineffective; they are forbidden to teach religious values and are often ridiculed for the ways they teach secular ones. The nuclear family, once the most basic institutional unit in our society, is under a strain that requires no elaborate explanation. At a historically alarming rate we are failing to maintain, and in many instances failing to form, traditional families.

This institutional weakness is doubtless a societal problem at all levels, but its effects are magnified in the condensed atmosphere of the city. The greater the heterogeneity in the population, the more obvious the absence of communication or mutual interest. Institutional weakness is most apparent in the inner city. When poverty and crime spotlight the plight of individuals, it is much easier to see how government or families or schools are ineffective carriers of individual character and social responsibility.

The majority of Americans are hesitant to request or accept a greatly expanded role for government. Most seem to prefer a reduced governmental role—the thrust of recent attempts at welfare reform. Although public funding may be required, there is considerable interest in strengthening the nongovernmental institutions of civil society.

It is against this backdrop that congregations are being asked to provide the services, the moral values, and the human networks for communication that can create both the individuals we would want as fellow citizens and the society in which we wish to live. Some harbor a nearly desperate hope that congregations can provide an institutional base for social life where other institutional bases are weak. This hope is just as real in the middle-class suburb as in the poorest inner-city neighborhood: everybody wants to belong to a community and to draw a sense of meaning from it. But where material needs are greater, the absence of socialization is more obvious.

Several insights have contributed to the rise of interest in congregations and their role in our communities. One is the conviction, offered most cogently by Peter Berger and R. J. Neuhaus (1977), that smaller, more local organizations serve as "mediating structures" that buffer individuals from the powerful and impersonal effects of the national state and the marketplace. Congregations, neighborhood organizations, and schools are all capable of serving this mediating function, but as is now clear, all three types of organizations have undergone changes that challenge their ability to perform this task effectively. Families are perhaps the mediating institution par excellence, but they operate at a much more personal, less public level and require some intermediate assistance.

A related insight was that our society seems to be missing, or perhaps losing, what James Coleman has described as "social capital." Robert Putnam's (1995a and b, 2001) celebrated use of the term highlighted the fear—one more in a long list of "declension" stories in America—that we are no longer joining and participating in civic organizations. The specific organizations that link our interests and opportunities no longer hold us, thus prompting the concern, since debated in innumerable ways, that we are a nation of isolated individuals.

Another important insight is that Americans have continued to think and behave religiously long after religion has receded as an authoritative institutional force in political or economic issues. White clergy, at least, are less important moral and political figures in their communities than was true just a few decades ago. Religion's influence has waned as a result of key battles in the war over the separation of church and state. Creationism and prayer have been discredited and disallowed in public schools. And yet individuals, at least a sizable portion, continue to both think and act religiously (Ammerman 2001).

A fourth insight, often associated with John McKnight and Jody Kretzmann (1993), is that community development might better proceed by focusing on assets available rather than on obvious deficiencies. This line of thinking has forced civic leaders to consider what a given place *has* rather than what it lacks; and, especially for poorer neighborhoods, religious congregations have been identified as important neighborhood assets, even if they are relatively weak in terms of budgets or programs.

Yet another important insight related to the idea of mediating structures is that congregations are especially important organizations for people who participate less in other forms of organizational life. Women, members of ethnic or racial minority groups, new immigrants, the elderly—many of these people participate in congregations more fully than in the polity or the marketplace. Congregations, as scholars such as Nancy Ammerman (1996, 1997) and Stephen Warner (1994) have argued, are the organizations where such people learn and hone organizational, bureaucratic, and leadership skills. Congregations are, so that thinking goes, the organizational base in which such people can operate at the center rather than always at the margins.

This confidence in congregations as social organizations, combined with a stifling recognition that other institutional bases are weak, has created renewed interest in congregations as civic actors. Many hope that congregations might be the institution, manifested in thousands of particular organizations, that can lend stability to an inherently unstable social situation. And the more unstable the social situation—especially in deteriorating inner cities—the greater the perceived need for congregations to step up to the task.

Renewed emphasis on congregations as civic actors is hardly universal. Religious studies scholars, especially those who have come to be associated with the field of congregational studies, continue to bemoan that other intellectual disciplines do not treat the institutional role of religion seriously enough. And they continue to be right. Neither historians nor sociologists, except those who specialize in religion, traditionally treat religious organizations as serious actors in their studies of urban or community life. Descriptions of inner-city life continue to reduce religion, if it is mentioned at all, to a surrogate for ethnicity or class. Although the field of congregational studies has blossomed, most scholarship on urban and community studies ignores religion. It would be fair to say that the bulk of urban scholarship has focused on national and transnational trends, both political and economic, that generate the dynamics of our lives together.

But even as rival camps in the intellectual world were honing their theoretical blades without much thought for religion, political and civic leaders have turned increasing attention toward the role of religious organizations. The new emphasis on congregations as community organizations came, not primarily from academe—although a few social scientists such as John DiIulio (1997a and b, 1999) developed an early interest—but from government agencies, schools, courts, and philanthropic foundations. Those who were turning to congregations and other faith-based groups saw institutional life, not as a variable to be explained, but as an asset to be built and used. They were interested in explaining the relative role of organizations only insofar as that explanation increases the effectiveness of those organizations in promoting common goods such as prosperity, freedom, or community—the latter usually broadly conceived as communication, trust, coordination, and cooperation.

It is these practitioners of civil society—politicians, community organizers, philanthropists, and the like—who have turned their attention to congregations as civic actors. The potential benefit of that turn is that the applied nature of the conversation will keep our thinking about it from devolving into so much theory and abstraction. But the potential cost is that relevant, critical questions will not be raised until it is too late. If congregations are being called upon to play a more vital role as civic actors, then we must ask at least three important questions.

First, what, specifically, is expected of congregations? As the professional practitioners of civil society turn toward them, what role do they have in mind? How are congregations to function as one of the "institutions of civil society"? Second, we must then ask, Are congregations able and willing to accept and perform the tasks that are being laid before them? Can they do what their proponents assume they can? Do they want to? Finally, we must ask, Will congregations themselves benefit from this role? This is a question that contains within it the enduring question of whether congregations could sustain this sort of activity. Will their other social roles and ministries change as they become more involved in community development and social services?

These are not questions with pat answers. As usual, the polarized sides in the debate provide little public benefit. Although a few conservatives may wish to turn the entire system of welfare and community development over to the churches as quickly as possible, this is not the mature view of responsible analysts or even of many politicians. Just as dangerous, surely, is the demagoguery of those who level such accusations at the political right without acknowledging that most people seek only a reasonable balance—as they define it—between public and private. Journalists who cite the same few tired examples of faith-based community development or social services provide little more help. They have filled the public arena with unrelated, unrepresentative, and unhelpful anecdotes.

Different people have different expectations for congregations' public roles. Because congregations vary so widely in type and size, surely their willingness and ability to become publicly engaged will also vary. In the same vein, it seems likely that some congregations will benefit by pursuing such a path and others will not.

Because the answers to those big questions are so variable—in one sense, the answer is always "it depends"—our goal here cannot be to make overly broad generalizations. Our goal, instead, is to think critically and systematically about the expectations and realities that underlie the trend toward increased congregational participation in civic life.

Because the issues raised here are driven by pragmatic applied concerns, the answer to these broad questions cannot be primarily theoretical. We must look at actual cases and ask: What stated and unstated assumptions or expectations drive the proposed new role for congregations? What activities have taken place and in what social context? What results are apparent, and what future results can be reasonably expected?

One problem with the current state of description of congregational roles is that it has been anecdotal in the worst sense of the word. Most of what we know about the role of congregations in public life has been described by people who have an obvious interest in strengthening that role. Political leaders, eager to demonstrate positive outcomes and perhaps to reduce the role played by government, point to the few highly successful examples of congregations delivering social services or generating a sense of local identity. Researchers, often paid by the same foundations and charities that support the community efforts of congregations and others, report the positive effects of congregations that would merit future support (both for the programs in questions and for the research). Congregations engaged in such activities trumpet their successes and downplay their failures in an effort to generate future moral and material support.

What we get in the national media, then, are litanies of examples that may be much more particular, and much less representative, than the authors are able to acknowledge. In an attempt to be broadly based, researchers and journalists have selected isolated examples that represent the trend they wish to describe but that could not possibly represent the full range of activities.

The approach of this book is nearly exactly opposite. We have focused almost all of our energy on understanding the role of religion in creating community life in Indianapolis. We have paid close attention to reports from Los Angeles, Chicago, Boston, Philadelphia, and New York and have engaged in some limited comparative analysis. Nonetheless, we have attempted to understand the entire range of religious and civic involvement in one city.

In following such an approach, we undoubtedly risk the possibility that Indianapolis is unique so that what we have learned here is not applicable elsewhere. Given that twice as many Americans live in cities with populations between 250,000 and one million as in megalopolises with populations over one million, the risk seems slim, but it is a risk we acknowledge and accept. We accept it because we believe the depth and breadth of our understanding of Indianapolis offers a perspective that no broader study that includes several cities could. We know enough of the history, polity, demography, regionalization, and cultural texture of Indianapolis to see the role of congregations in civic life in a light not generally available.

In the course of our research, I served as an unpaid adviser or proposal evaluator for most of the early efforts to involve congregations in civic life. I worked with the mayor's office, the juvenile court, the Coalition for Homelessness Intervention and Prevention, the Indiana Youth Institute, and Indiana's Family and Social Services Administration as they were just starting experiments using congregations as partners in social reforms.

Crucial information about religion in urban areas is hard to get. Many of the civic leaders proposing these reforms knew relatively little about differences among Catholics and Protestants, among congregations of different races, or about the general religious demography of the city. My job was often to provide some of that context for them.

By being involved, I subjected myself to the risk that my conclusions would be colored by my personal feelings about those with whom I worked, their clients, or the nature of their organizations. However, I consider it a much greater risk that without my involvement, our research would have been of little benefit to them. It is in that spirit that this book is written.

## Changing Expectations

The new expectations about the role of congregations in civic life described above have developed gradually but unmistakably over the course of the last decade. The 1998 announcement of a new initiative within the Department of Housing and Urban Development (HUD) highlighted those changes, but the move only solidified a trend that was well underway. Former HUD Secretary Henry Cisneros was trumpeting the role of congregations in urban community building well before the creation of that new department and a full five years before dust was kicked up by President George W. Bush's "Armies of Compassion" (2001).

In his essay "Higher Ground" (1996), Cisneros beat the drum for what he called "faith communities" in the inner city. He made the institutional poverty of the inner city and the perceived ability of congregations to mitigate that poverty unambiguously clear:

> The youth left behind (in the inner city) were deprived of role models, exposure to the world of work, and linkages to social institutions and friendship networks. Add the crack epidemic and the easy availability of firearms and there is little wonder that gang violence and other scourges emerged.
>
> But this essay is not about pessimism. Quite the contrary, it is about the remarkable hope being rekindled in communities across America. Faith communities are at the center of this good work.

Cisneros went on to list four features that allow faith communities to offer hope to inner cities in a way that no other institution can match. Other institutions, he suggested, may have some combination of these, but only faith communities have all four. First, *faith communities are still there.* They are physically present in threatened neighborhoods. Second, *community is central to the mission of charity; and congregations, one is led to assume, emphasize the community in their good works.* Third, *faith communities have unique resources,* especially the resource of people who can organize and mobilize support. Finally, *faith communities touch the soul.* They offer "values and moral structure" that meet needs of inner-city dwellers whose problems "go far beyond simple lack of material wealth."

Cisneros's list is not exhaustive, but it begins to capture something of the expectations created for congregations. The general sense that congregations could do something well was boosted by the corresponding sense that other institutions had failed. One need not argue that congregations provide a panacea or that their efforts are without conflict or problem if one has already determined that the alternatives are untenable.

It is this latter thrust that supports much of the rhetoric about the role of congregations in the city. Whether one promotes a limited or an expansive version of what congregations can do, their possibilities look greater against the backdrop of "nothing else works." This is especially true when thinking about options for at-risk youth in inner-city neighborhoods. As a White House aide put it, "I don't know if we've reached this point because these (religious) programs have succeeded or because everything else has failed, but this certainly seems to be the hot social-policy topic these days."

One of the earliest proponents of faith-based alternatives to social work was John DiIulio of Princeton University. Long before he went to work in the Bush administration, he echoed Cisneros when saying,

> Churches are critical to the effort [to save a generation of youth] because they alone are capable of addressing both the material and the spiritual dimensions of the problem.
> What the churches are capable of doing, I think uniquely, is looking at the whole range of problems that surround these at-risk children. They are also capable of doing it in a way that is unapologetic about the unconditional love that motivates it. (1997)

The most compelling virtue of congregations as community builders and service providers, according to this reasoning, is that they do what they do in the context of love and charity. They are motivated by faith and by strong moral values, and those values are ostensibly transmitted in the provision of services and in the joining together of common interests.

Underlying moral values are not, however, the only expectations that drive the turn toward congregations as community institutions. There is a basic assumption that congregations are local organizations and that they have specific local knowledge that makes them better able to serve the specific needs of their neighbors.

One way of expressing this local priority is Cisneros's claim that faith-based community organizing is "driven from the bottom up." Because congregations are imagined to be local organizations as opposed to federal or state-based ones, they are part of the mix in which "communities organize themselves. And these self-organized, grass-roots ventures, "establish true partnerships across institutions and between institutions and residents, and play a commanding role in designing and implementing . . . strategies" (1996:14).

Contrary to some media images, then, the Bush administration did not create the federal government's interest in congregations as centers of community building and social services, nor were they first to recommend public funding for such work. They simply upped the ante by suggesting that the nascent partnerships between government and faith-based groups could be expanded and that public funding could be enhanced. This line of thinking was not essentially different from that of the Clinton administration:

> Government cannot be replaced by charities, but it can and should welcome them as partners. We must heed the growing consensus across America that successful government and social programs work in fruitful partnership with community-serving and faith-based organizations—whether run by Methodists, Muslims, Mormons, or good people of no faith at all. (Bush 2001)

Embedded in that "growing consensus" about partnerships across institutions, and between institutions and residents, is the subtle assumption that congregations are savvy, street-wise members of the neighborhoods that surround their houses of worship. There is a deep hope, especially among those concerned about inner-city neighborhoods, that congregations understand the motives and speak the language of the people who most need help.

One way to express this expectation is to say that many believe that congregations are *local* organizations. Congregations, in this view, know about and cooperate with other local organizations, including community development groups, neighborhood associations, and other congregations. But there is an even deeper assumption: that congregations also know the faces and emotions of the individuals who live nearby. Congregations are not simply part of the organizational network, what we might call the institutional infrastructure of a community, but they also have intimate knowledge of the residents that other organizations (especially imagined impersonal welfare bureaucrats) do not have. The language of "neighborhood" dominates the rhetoric:

> Federal policy should reject the failed formula of towering, distant bureaucracies that too often prize process over performance.
> . . . Faith-based and grassroots organizations do not always perform miracles. Together, however, they are a vitally important resource in our communities, reaching out to needy neighbors and neighborhoods in thousands of ways. (Bush 2001)

Because so much energy is being directed at and expected from congregations based on assumptions about their rootedness in particular places, it is strange that so few have asked whether these assumptions are descriptively valid. Do congregations draw their members from the surrounding neighborhood? Do pastors or members know the neighbors who live around their house of worship? Are congregations linked to the other organizations that undergird community life? These are the sorts of descriptive questions that should be answered before proceeding on the assumption that congregations have an advantage over other social-service or community-building groups based on their connections to place.

Another expectation, too little articulated or challenged, is that congregations can function effectively as community organizations with relatively little administrative or bureaucratic overhead. This notion follows the age-old Catholic principle of subsidiarity in the assumption that the smallest, most local level of organization capable of carrying out a task should do so. Put another way, organizations and administrative structures should be no larger and no farther from the area of concern than they must be.

Although the term *subsidiarity* is out of vogue, the principle itself has become so commonsensical that it serves no useful purpose to dissect it here. Devolution is a way of life in American policy. But how the principle of subsidiarity applies to congregations as community builders and service providers is an important question and worthy of further reflection. The question is not whether congregations have administrative or bureaucratic bloat, because most surely do not. The question is whether this says more about the nature of congregations as organizations or more about their relatively small size and small scope of activities in comparison to other organizations.

Congregations, like other small organizations, may be able to provide services or develop community ties in relatively small, carefully defined ways without much administrative overhead. But could many of these congregations, or even all of them, cover the entire range of service needs with each working locally on a small scale? Or viewed from the other side of the equation, are community needs too large to be addressed piecemeal by a myriad of organizations working without centralized control?

This line of questioning applies both to the community-building and the welfare service provision aspects of congregational civic involvement. There can be no doubt, however, that recent attention has focused more on social services in the arena usually termed "welfare reform."

The legal change that has done the most to highlight the role of congregations as social welfare service providers is Section 104 of the Personal Responsibility and Work Opportunity Reconciliation Act of 1996. Section 104, usually referred to as "Charitable Choice," allows faith-based organizations to compete with other "vendors" in open bidding to deliver welfare services. Put another way, if any private organization can contract with the state to deliver welfare services, then faith-based organizations may compete also. Most importantly, faith-based organizations cannot be prevented from practicing and discussing their faith in the provision of those services.

The section included, as one might expect, a host of requirements and provisions. Most importantly, the law as written originally applied only to block grants made to states under the Temporary Assistance to Needy Families (TANF) program, though it has since been expanded to cover certain other areas such as Welfare to Work, Community Services Block Grants, and some drug treatment programs. Furthermore, states are not required to deal with private vendors at all. They can still choose to deliver services solely through governmental entities. The provision states only that if they allow any private contractors to bid on services, then they must allow faith-based organizations to bid as well.

Congregations and religious nonprofit groups can still practice their faith and even discuss it, but they cannot make membership in their group a condition or requirement for any client they serve. Moreover, any client has the right to refuse to have services delivered by a faith-based group, and a secular one must be provided if they do.

Despite these provisions, however, the change in the law is still dramatic. For certain pools of money, congregations and other religious organizations can compete freely without having to neuter their programs of religious referents. Congregations can propose social services that promote religious values and ideas to those who receive other services if the recipients so desire. For the many people who promote the role of congregations precisely because of their faith and value commitments, this was a historic legal precedent.

Changes that were begun immediately in the George W. Bush administration followed this same line of reasoning. They were changes in degree, not changes in type. The new president made it clear that he believed in the principles embodied in the Charitable Choice laws and wished to press that same logic into every branch of federal government involved in welfare or community development funding. Toward that end he appointed John DiIulio, who served only very briefly, to head a White House office with a mandate to increase funding to those institutions of civil society, especially "faith-based organizations." He also appointed former Indianapolis Mayor Stephen Goldsmith to head the Corporation for National Service with a new mandate to look for every opportunity to increase participation in social service provision among religious groups.

The new administration ratcheted up the expectation that religious groups, especially religious congregations, could function as effective social organizations. Those expectations were based on the same assumptions first made by Cisneros during his days at HUD.

## Three Basic Assumptions

For some purposes it would be necessary to keep "community building," "development of social capital," and "delivery of social services" analytically distinct. They are, after all, not really the same. Some organizations and some activities may be very good at engendering trust and communication but lack the desire or resources to deliver social services. Similarly, some groups or activities may deliver services efficiently but lack the interpersonal connections necessary to build community.

Although these distinctions do matter, and this book will refer to them from time to time, it is not necessary to draw a hard philosophical line between them at this juncture precisely because the practitioners who advocate the social potency of congregations do not make rigid distinctions. Indeed, although the Cisneros essay was titled "Faith Communities and Community Building," much of the essay was about economic development, housing development, or welfare service provision. Conversely, people who talk about the virtue of congregations as service providers point to their strengths as community builders in the process.

One early study of the role of congregations in community development set out to evaluate several organizational partnerships that had been funded by the Lilly Endowment. Those partnerships sought to mix congregations with other secular and religious organizations to promote economic development, which is essentially a social service activity. What the evaluators found was that the most important resources offered by congregations were moral support and political clout. That is, their greatest contribution to these economic development efforts was their ability to generate community goodwill and support around them (Lilly Endowment 1994).

Social services and community building do not always need to be analytically separated, because *their interplay is at the heart of the argument for the effectiveness of congregations.* The force of the arguments for congregations as partners and providers in the urban setting comes from the claim that social services and community development should not proceed without communication, trust, and the presence of strong moral values. Good values make good services; good community makes good community development. The practitioners have forged a link between the spirit of community and the infrastructure of community that is meant to be interdependent and indissoluble.

Those who champion congregations as community builders and service deliverers operate on the three basic assumptions described below. Not all of them share all three; some are more the province of the political left, and some more the province of the right. But there are three distinct assumptions about the role of congregations in community life, and especially in inner city community life, that make the arguments for congregations as community-building institutions most plausible.

The first assumption, common to the political right, left, and center, is that *congregations possess important local knowledge that allows them to deal more effectively with local circumstances.* The assumption is virtually axiomatic: community is particular, it is about these people with these assets and these needs, and congregations are best able to address the community because they know the details.

The second assumption is that *congregations specifically, and faith-based organizations more generally, provide services with the least interference from bureaucracy or regulation.* This assumption is linked to the principle of subsidiarity, the notion that every activity should be governed at the smallest, most local level of organization that is capable of performing the needed task.

The third assumption, and in many ways the most fervently held, is that *congregations, and indeed all faith-based organizations, bring moral teachings and strong core values to bear on whatever service or community-building activities they undertake.* In the social service world, as in the academic world, there is a huge debate between those who associate some forms of poverty with moral failure—they distinguish between the "deserving" and "undeserving" poor—and those who look toward structural causes. Most welfare reformers, though, see material poverty married to spiritual poverty, which is why they believe faith-based organizations are uniquely positioned to combat the two together. The "value-added" that makes congregations attractive as the institutional center of community life is that they "add values" to essentially secular activities.

These three assumptions all deal with the relationship of the congregation to its surrounding environment. In each of these, the environment is the dependent variable. The question is: What is the role and the capacity of congregations, with respect to community building of all types, within that environment? Although this book will continually challenge the prima facie validity of all three assumptions, it will not in any way argue that they are simply false. In some cases, congregations do have useful local knowledge. In given instances, administrative flexibility is crucial. In many ways, as everyone knows, congregations do transmit religious and ethical values.

What this book will argue, however, is that each of these assumptions must be put to the test in very specific local contexts. Both public policy and grant making are proceeding from general assumptions that are inadequately applied to important differences in environments. What congregations want, what they are capable of, and what the community needs or expects from them in real life is much more dependent on social context than is generally acknowledged.

There is one more set of assumptions about the congregations themselves and about their internal interests to which the book eventually returns. The notion of faith communities as community builders has implications for the congregations themselves quite independently of the role they do or might play in the community. One cannot ask only about the positive or negative effects on the *environment* when congregations participate. At some point, one must ask what happens to the *congregations* as expectations of them change.

The practitioners who have generated the interest in congregations as important community institutions have done so with the secular neighborhood community in mind. They are interested in building social capital, in keeping young people on the straight and narrow, and in building communities full of better-housed, better-employed individuals. Their view of congregations can be simple and benign: "Some congregations already want to help in these tasks, and others might be convinced to help. If they can do it better than alternative groups, then let's get out of their way."

But as congregations hear the call to be community builders, they too will have to consider whether and how to heed it. They too should consider the assumptions and their relationship to real events couched in their full social context.

There have now been many accounts, first in journalism (Klein 1997; Shapiro 1996) and now emerging in the scholarly literature, about the role of the religious community in welfare reform (Cnaan, Wineburg, and Boddie 2000; Wineburg 2000; Sherman 2000; Ramsay 1998; Farnsley 2000; Farnsley 2001a and b). Although quantitative data about faith-based welfare reform has been scant, Mark Chaves and others have turned a statistical eye on congregations as potential service providers (Chaves 1998; 2001; Chaves and Tsitsos 2001). There is also a substantial body of work on religious community development and a burgeoning field of congregational studies.

In evaluating faith-based reforms, caution is required because the big questions are not, after all, about whether some congregations and some individuals can do a good job as community builders or service providers. Everyone knows the answer already: some can and some will. A decade ago, it was important to highlight public understanding about the multitude of benefits congregations provided for their communities because those contributions were often overlooked. Academic disdain for religion may continue, but civic leaders are no longer overlooking religion. Anyone who does not realize how much congregations do both for their members and for the broader community is just not paying attention.

Congregations will continue to do great good, but it is not clear which ones will take on the added role of partnering with public institutions in the interest of strengthening civil society. Those who want to put public funds into the community through congregations or to count on congregations as community organizations with multiple secular responsibilities need to ask difficult questions about the kinds of congregations likely to be involved and their capacity for effectiveness.

This last point about difficult questions cannot be overstated. To some, the tone of this book may seem unduly critical of congregations. It is, in many ways, an argument that many congregations *cannot* meet the rising expectations placed before them, or it is at least an argument for extreme caution. Promoters of greater religious involvement will find this pessimistic. Would it not be better, some will argue, to emphasize what congregations *can* do and to focus on their many accomplishments? Is it not better to focus on assets and strengths, as McKnight and Kretzmann (1993) have done, rather than to repeat weaknesses and liabilities?

The problem here is a real one. Those who study religion and those philanthropic funders who promote religious institutions and religious values have an ongoing interest in showing how congregations are more important and more effective in community building than many scholars or politicians had previously given them credit for. Those who study local religion often find themselves arguing for the influence of religion in the face of analyses that focus primarily on economic or political factors. Both students of religion and promoters of religion must always argue against the reductionism that discounts religious practice.

Students of religion will generally agree that the religious dimension of life has frequently been slighted in historical or sociological analysis. Moreover, most are keenly aware of the many contributions congregations make to the lives of their members and to the broader community; however, as noted above, a growing body of literature on congregations and their social implications makes that a poorly kept secret. Nothing contained in this book is meant to discount the enormous contributions made by communities of faith to American public life.

That said, however, there is a great difference between claiming that congregations deserve our intellectual attention and even our public gratitude, and claiming that we ought to be optimistic about their ability to meet new public expectations about their social roles. Having watched developments in Indianapolis very closely for several years and having read widely in the growing field of congregational literature, it is clear to me that overestimating the capacities of congregations poses many threats, not the least of which will be sincere disappointment. If we significantly change the provision of social services based on faulty assumptions, we run the risk of leaving aid recipients in need and of damaging a fragile service infrastructure. If we count on these organizations to rebuild our sense of civic community and they do not have the capacity to do so, then we risk the opportunity cost of not developing other areas that were more promising. If we ask congregations as organizations to do what they cannot, we risk damaging their capacity to do what they can do effectively.

There is, in some circles, almost a sense of desperation. We turn to congregations because, as the government official quoted above lamented, "nothing else works." But any such act has serious risks, including the opportunity costs associated with the paths *not* chosen and the arrival of unintended consequences. Without belittling what congregations can do, we must ask several key questions before we move too far in the direction of a significant institutional realignment.

Do congregations know more about their social environments, or can they better transmit positive social values, than other organizations? What is the relationship between the scope of social need and the capacity of interested congregations to meet it? How is congregational activity in this realm tied to specific neighborhood or environmental circumstances? What kinds of congregations tend toward community involvement, and what kinds avoid it? Finally, what happens to congregations that join the community development fray?

These questions require answers, and no recounting of heroic stories about particular congregations will answer them. Moreover, no simple set of survey questions, no matter how widely asked, will capture the crucial contextual nuances.

That is why this book intends to offer observations from one city where experiments involving congregations in a variety of new partnerships and programs are already underway. The goal is not to tell congregations what they should or should not be doing. The goal, instead, is to describe what is really happening in the sort of contextual setting that can only be viewed when one has the luxury of observing a wide range of activities in their broader social environment over an extended period.

The time to ask whether congregations *should* be involved in partnerships with government or with secular foundations is past. Similarly, it no longer makes sense to ask whether sweeping changes in social welfare thinking will cause an organizational realignment. It probably does not even make sense to ask whether congregations should be touted as producers of social capital. These movements are already underway.

It makes more sense now to ask: What sort of contextual information do congregations, foundations, nonprofit groups, and local governments need to consider as they build new partnerships? As each of these groups plunges forward, how can they best understand the nature of the steps they are taking? Finally, what are reasonable and realistic expectations about the role congregations can play?

Recounting observations from Indianapolis and analyzing the relevant details should prove useful both to civic and to religious leaders as they think about their future choices. The choices made by any group must be made with a realistic assessment of what already exists and what is possible.

# 2  Congregations as Urban Organizations

> We can think about a community in which a congregation is lodged as an
> ecology of resources and organizations in which people seek out social sup-
> port for everything from the most basic survival needs to sociability, aesthetic
> pleasure, meaning making and community improvement. To understand what
> is happening in a community, in fact, it may be more useful to observe the
> stock of skills and connections it comprises than to inventory the organiza-
> tions themselves. (Ammerman et al. 1997)

If local communities and their institutions are to assess the role of faith-based
organizations accurately, they must begin by thinking about the specific contextual details that shape their social environment. One of the greatest mistakes
made by community groups—from local governments, to nonprofit organizations, to congregations—is that each tends to see its activities in a vacuum. In a
survey of faith-based youth programs in Indianapolis, for instance, we found
that roughly 80 percent of service providers believed that the programs offered
by their organization were unique. In fact, most were substantially identical to,
but thoroughly detached from, other similar programs.

We live in a mass-production society. A suburban commercial strip of road
on the south side of Indianapolis looks very much like any similar strip on the
north, west, or east side: the same fast food restaurants, the same shopping out-
lets, the same gas stations. More remarkable, though for most of us it has ceased
to be astonishing, is the fact that the suburban commercial strip on the south
side of Atlanta or Nashville or Pittsburgh looks much the same as those of the
south side of Indianapolis.

These mass-produced similarities, coupled with the federal government's
mandate to find solutions to problems faced all across a population of 280 million people, often lead to policies that seem to assume that "one size fits all."
Unfortunately, however, even as they attempt to tailor a custom fit, too many
reformers still see inner-city culture and the congregations that inhabit them as
cut from the same cloth.

American society is, in fact, characterized by some very real differences in
local and regional culture. On a number of issues—gun control and animal
rights are excellent examples—enormous, crucial differences between rural and
urban interests make national debate very difficult to sustain.

Part of the logic of welfare reform is, after all, that state governments—and by extension the local governments within them—understand local needs better than the federal government run from Washington ever could. There is an understandable bias toward the local in devolution. But those who would devolve services cannot simply assume that smaller organizations are "local" in the sense of being indigenous or tied to grass-roots concentrations of information and resources. Any organizations considering faith-based partnerships in community development and welfare reform must pay particular attention to the social context in which their activities would unfold. They must consider the social setting and relevant history, the political environment, the religious environment, and the other service groups already participating. As they consider each of these variables at the local level, they must try to set them in the context of the larger national picture.

A number of sociologists have advocated an "ecological" approach to understanding religious organizations (Milofsky 1988, 1997; Ammerman et al. 1997; Eiesland 2000). Put most simply, religious organizations, like any others, exist in a complex ecology that includes many different elements. Any organization—as any organism in a biological model—must pick and choose among the available resources in order to get what it needs to survive, or else it gradually becomes extinct. When resources are scarce, organizations compete for them.

One advantage of such a model is that it broadens the available view of religious organizations as a whole. It is easy to look at any given congregation or any given tradition and see that it is waxing or waning, but it is difficult, and even dangerous, to infer too much from that. An ecological perspective allows the viewer to take a step back and ask: Which organizations are thriving and which are declining? The ecological model calls for some very hard work, however, because it requires the viewer to look at many different factors at the same time. To understand any organization or any policy in full ecological context, it is necessary to think critically about the many elements that make up its context.

Partners in faith-based reforms need not become sociologists or urban planning analysts, but they do need to ask themselves some hard questions about the particular environments they inhabit. What works in one set of ecological conditions may not work in others; what works one place may not work elsewhere. The logic of faith-based reforms is that local organizations, often congregations, can provide custom-fit solutions to local problems. Unless the planners consider the many variables at work in the local ecology, however, they will continue the flawed policy of trying to make one size fit all, even if the "one size" is now offered at the local rather than the national level. Such a strategy may work for hamburger stands, but it does not work for policies meant to increase social integration and self-sufficiency.

## The National Political Context

Clearly, the national setting is ripe for faith-based partnerships. President Bush made it clear early in his administration that every federal agency will now follow the basic guidelines set up in the 1996 concept of Charitable Choice. The U.S. Congress and the courts may have other ideas, but the principle is in place (Carlson-Theis 1997, 2000).

Perhaps even more important than any of these specific items, however, are three national trends. The first is a pronounced tendency toward devolution that the Bush administration wishes to expand. Americans seem to favor *returning control of resources from the federal government to the states and, where possible, from the states toward even greater local control*. Cities are designing programs meant to boost neighborhoods and to make policing and recreation more local matters.

This trend toward local control fits hand-in-glove with the second trend, which is to *emphasize supportive communities rather than material assistance provided case-by-case to individuals*. Both community development and welfare reform provide excellent examples of this. In welfare reform, there is a growing recognition that simply giving people money does not always alleviate their poverty. What the poor need, at least in some instances, is the stable, supportive community that sees people through the rough periods in their lives. Welfare is still delivered to individuals, of course, but there is a new linkage between these individuals and their communities. For one thing, the provider of the services is more likely to live locally and be somewhat more attuned to local circumstance—or at least that is the hope. For another, community development is focusing on building local institutions—schools, stores, recreation facilities, even jobs—capable of supporting the neighbors. It is no accident that welfare reform is occurring at the same time that forced busing is ending and neighborhood schools are on the rise.

A third trend, hailed by some and decried by others, is toward privatization, or at least *toward an expanded role for private organizations in public-private partnerships*. Few in American politics argue that welfare and neighborhood renewal and economic expansion can be entirely disassociated from federal or at least state government planning. But there is growing recognition—President Bush calls it a "growing consensus"—shared on both the political right and the left, that some new combination of public and private is both desirable and possible. For welfare reformers, this means arrangements in which private providers, even sectarian religious providers, might be supported by public funds under certain conditions. It also means that some of the nation's enormous foundations, such as the Lilly Endowment or Pew Charitable Trusts or the Ford Foundation—may fund ventures involving local government, secular providers, and sectarian providers in the same scheme. Civil libertarians may wince at the thought, but a new alignment of interests is evolving.

The national stage is thus set for faith-based reforms. Because that setting involves considerable devolution to state and local governments, however, the nuances of regional and local ecologies become all the more important. Partners in these new reforms must consider the details that make their place what it is, because those details are likely to determine the outcome of any service experiments.

One of the key elements to consider first in any more local ecology is the role played by state and local government. At present, the welfare funds designated as Temporary Assistance for Needy Families (TANF) are distributed in block grants to the states. Under Charitable Choice, each state can choose to spend this money as it wishes. If it means to provide all services itself with its own employees, it can do so. The religious factor in Charitable Choice kicks in, however, at the point where states decide to contract some of their services. If a state chooses to contract with any private providers, then it must let faith-based providers compete equally and must not discriminate against them because of any overt religious activity. Put another way, states cannot discriminate against churches or synagogues because they display religious symbols or because they use specific faith commitments to determine their hiring practices. These are the sorts of changes that separate Charitable Choice from previous legal arrangements detailing cooperation between church and state.

To date, states have chosen one of three paths. The first path is to proceed as usual without any change in stance toward religious organizations. Some states simply do not deal with private contractors and thus save themselves the additional task of having to make sure their funding competitions are fair and open within the bounds of changing legislation. In such an environment, faith-based partnerships are unlikely to thrive because there is no impetus for congregations to change their own status quo, no new resources available in the environment that they might use to their advantage.

A second path is for states to strive for complete objectivity. It is certainly possible for state government, or local governments dealing with their states, to take the view that religious groups can compete freely and will not suffer discrimination, as outlined in the 1996 legislation, but to insist that religious organizations will receive no preferable treatment. Faith-based partnerships can succeed in such an environment, but two factors militate against them. One factor is that most congregations and many religious traditions are new to the process of writing grants, administering funds, or evaluating programs, a point we will return to in chapter 5. Given this lack of experience, they are at a considerable disadvantage against established secular programs or even against established religious efforts such as Catholic Charities that know the ropes and have established bureaucratic channels.

The other factor militating against congregations is that most are either unfamiliar with, or uneasy about, Charitable Choice. If the goal is simply to provide them fair access, then there is little reason to think that many of them will seize the initiative. The costs involved in writing grants or going to planning meetings are high, especially for organizations with no spare capacity in professional leadership. The cost of possible regulatory interference by government or foundations in their ministries is also high. The benefits, when one factors in the true likelihood of receiving funding, are relatively low. Therefore, in a genuinely neutral environment, most congregations and many denominations or larger religious traditions will largely stay put.

A third path taken by some states is open promotion of an expanded role for faith-based organizations. The impetus for this promotional role seems to be twofold. On the one hand, some government officials genuinely favor the faith-based option and want to do all they can to strengthen it. On the other hand, some who are suspicious of increased faith-based involvement do not want the issue used against them at the polls, so they are touting changes and new opportunities though secretly hoping that not too much will come of the changes. Moreover, even those who are suspicious of an enlarged role for the faith community fear lawsuits. As in civil rights cases, they want to guarantee that they are not discriminating against faith-based groups; and toward that end, they are offering new training and special programs designed to encourage their participation or at least hold off any legal claim that they have somehow discouraged it.

## The Local Political Context

In Indianapolis, local government seized the initiative in faith-based reform. Stephen Goldsmith, who was mayor until the end of 1999, began the Front Porch Alliance as a way to involve local community groups in his ongoing program of Building Better Neighborhoods. Mayor Goldsmith hired a director and engaged a staff to work with local community groups, but their primary charge was to act as a sort of hotline for churches and other religious groups needing help from city hall. Through the Front Porch Alliance (FPA), Mayor Goldsmith provided some resources to these groups in the form of local grants, but more often he provided moral and technical support as they applied for other grants. The FPA disseminated information about funding opportunities and even went so far as to use staff time to help congregations write more effective applications.

Perhaps most important of all, though, Mayor Goldsmith used the bully pulpit of his office to spur congregations to greater action. He brought in Rev. Eugene Rivers of Boston to trumpet the success of that city's Ten Point Coalition. He highlighted the efforts of local religious leaders and called on others to do the same. He set a tone that suggested not merely that religious organizations could compete as equals with other organizations but even that religious organizations were *preferable* service options that justified the city's attempts to encourage and increase their participation.

Mayor Goldsmith was not the only local official in Indianapolis to undertake such an experiment. Marion County Juvenile Court Judge James Payne also turned to religious providers. The county organization that funds the court began contracting with a few religious counseling centers and with several urban pastors to serve as providers of "home-based counseling" to juveniles who received that sentence.

Judge Payne's reasoning was clear. He said he was paying millions for social services and getting unsatisfactory results. He believed he would do no worse with religious counselors, and might do better. Several hundred families have now been assigned to religious caseworkers, often African-American pastors, as part of their sentence. Although the Charitable Choice legislation does not govern the activities of the juvenile court, the same principles have been applied. Families are free to choose secular alternatives, though at least during the program's early stages, they were encouraged to consider the advantages of the faith-based options.

A third program, funded with foundation money rather than public funds, was also part of the change toward the new partnerships. The Coalition for Homelessness Intervention and Prevention (CHIP) received a substantial grant from the Lilly Endowment to be provided through the local United Way. With a portion of this money, approximately $500,000, CHIP intended to involve congregations as partners in transitional housing.

All applicants for the CHIP program had to provide some sort of sustainable transitional housing and had to include some significant role played by a local congregation or congregations. From the congregations that initially applied, five would be granted $10,000 to continue their planning and write a more detailed proposal. From these, three would receive substantial grants of up to $150,000.

The CHIP initiative is significant for two reasons. First, it upped the stakes in faith-based reform in the city. $150,000 is a considerable sum, more than the average congregation's annual budget. Second, it represented the city's premier philanthropic force, Lilly Endowment Incorporated, making a significant venture into the faith-based fray.

## The Social Context of Indianapolis

In some ways, the initiatives undertaken in Indianapolis were direct products of the city's historical development. Indianapolis is a large Midwestern city and the capital of Indiana. It is a major urban area, home to the Indianapolis 500, sports teams in both the National Football League (NFL) and the National Basketball Association (NBA), and one of the nation's largest charitable foundations, the Lilly Endowment.

Although it is a big city with a population of about 850,000 in the city itself and about one and a half million in the metropolitan area, Indianapolis is certainly not a megalopolis. It is unlike the major metropolises of New York, Los Angeles, Miami, or Chicago, most notably because it lacks the racial and ethnic mix that characterizes those larger cities. In Los Angeles, for instance, no ethnic group—including whites—constitutes a majority. By such comparisons, Indianapolis is relatively homogeneous.

Nearly three-fourths of the residents of Indianapolis proper are white. If one counts the entire metropolitan area, that figure is closer to 90 percent, owing to the virtually all-white suburban counties. Most of the remaining quarter of the city's population is black. All other ethnic groups combined account for no more than 3 to 5 percent of the total population.

Indianapolis also lacks obvious ethnic neighborhoods. Although the city was settled by German and Irish immigrants, there are no longer any neighborhoods that are solidly and recognizably German or Irish, although there are certainly places where those cultural backgrounds are strongly felt. The same could be said for Italians or eastern Europeans.

Although there has been a significant rise in Hispanic residents during the 1990s, especially transplants from Mexico, there is no barrio in Indianapolis. There are neighborhoods with more Mexican restaurants or groceries, but no place where one expects the majority of billboards or storefront signs to be in Spanish. In order to understand the dynamics of inner-city life in Indianapolis or the role of congregations therein, it is necessary to know a little more about how Indianapolis developed as an urban center and how religious life developed within it.

It is impossible to understand contemporary Indianapolis apart from the concept of "Unigov." Like many American cities, Indianapolis was confronted during the 1950s and 1960s with the realization that many of the city's citizens —the people who worked downtown and used city services—did not live within the city limits. Unlike other American cities, however, Indianapolis made legal changes that brought the virtually all of Marion County, roughly a twenty mile by twenty mile square with Indianapolis proper at its center, into the city limits.

On the one hand, the newly united city and county government, or Unigov, solved some of the "free rider" problems posed by suburbanites. At the least, it made being a free rider more costly by expanding the limits of who was inside and who was outside. Many of the people who worked downtown, went to ball games and museums downtown, and used city streets and police protection, now paid local taxes downtown. To live "outside," one has to live much farther from the center. On the other hand, Unigov significantly affected racial political balance. Blacks made up a sizable percentage of the population in the old city limits, but they were a much smaller slice of the new pie. Although the Seventh District, covering downtown Indianapolis and some of the suburbs, has a black congresswoman, Indianapolis has never had a black mayor. In fact, the 1999 election saw the first Democratic mayor since the creation of Unigov.

Whatever one's view of Unigov as a political system, it was not a social panacea. For one thing, many suburbanites or would-be suburbanites simply moved out to the surrounding counties, commuting even longer distances to work downtown. The growth of the interstate highway system, nearly coincidental with Unigov, made that commuting distance tolerable. For another thing, a few independent towns within the county refused to be fully annexed. The towns of Speedway, where the famous track is located, and Lawrence, then home to Fort Benjamin Harrison, continued to elect their own mayors and hire their own police, though they also participated in the county-wide governance structure.

Following the implementation of Unigov and court-ordered busing, many white Indianapolis residents, and a number of middle-class or wealthier black residents, headed for the townships. The inner-city schools, already under pressure because of a relatively poor and less well-educated population, came under even greater pressure.

A federal court order in 1971 made some changes in the segregation of schools, but in a fashion that is almost unfathomable to nonresidents of Indianapolis. That order bused selected black students from Indianapolis Public Schools out to the township schools to achieve racial balance and to assure educational equity. The order did not, however, bus any students from the townships back into Indianapolis Public Schools. Those schools, not surprisingly, lost enrollment rapidly, making the already difficult burden heavier still.

Indianapolis has had its share of de-industrialization common to all Midwestern cities in the so-called Rust Belt. It has seen the development of homogeneous edge cities and the movement of remaining industry, including new high-tech jobs, to the periphery of the city. Like all cities, it has seen changes to the inner city linked to the dual factors of race and schools. But in Indianapolis, clear political, systemic changes underscored those other demographic movements. When one considers the assets and vulnerabilities in inner-city Indianapolis, it is important to keep the contours of those movements in mind.

Indianapolis prides itself on being a city with little overt racial and ethnic tension. During the Great Society years, Indianapolis steadfastly refused federal aid to build public housing. Consequently, it has nothing one would refer to as a large "housing project" with all the negative stereotypes associated therewith, although it certainly has apartment complexes that are subsidized through public assistance. In fact, many of the poor in Indianapolis live in, or at least share, single-family dwellings in the inner city.

Indianapolis has experienced relatively little overt tension, either during the race riots that swept America in the late sixties and early seventies or during the so-called Rodney King riots of the early 1990s.

Indianapolis, like Indiana as a whole, enjoyed a very low rate of unemployment throughout the 1990s, although the rate is much higher in some inner-city neighborhoods. It created many manufacturing and service jobs. Although it is developing some high-technology industry as all cities are, Indianapolis has not created a software or engineering corridor. Few really large companies are headquartered in Indianapolis. Lilly, the pharmaceutical giant, is easily the largest; although many businesses, such as the Big Three automakers, have manufacturing facilities here. What one finds in Indianapolis, as in the state as a whole, is that most people are working and earning a living wage. Few people, however, are employed in the high-paying, high-tech fields one might find in the booming suburbs of Atlanta or Chicago.

Educational statistics about Indiana help illuminate this "middle position." Although Indiana is in the upper half of the fifty states in the percentages of residents who earn high school diplomas and in high school graduates who go on to earn baccalaureate degrees, it is forty-seventh in percentage of residents over the age of twenty-five who have baccalaureate degrees. Clearly, Indiana is not drawing, or even keeping, the best and brightest. It is, instead, supporting a strong, working middle class with relatively little poverty and relatively little affluence relative to the rest of the nation. Indianapolis reflects the white, working-class nature of the state.

Even this brief introduction to the city would not be complete without a few more words about Lilly Endowment Incorporated, which at this writing is second only to the Gates Foundation in terms of available assets. Created from the Lilly family's personal fortunes and nearly wholly invested in Eli Lilly pharmaceutical stock, the Endowment, as it is called locally, is a major player in Indianapolis life. Many people across the country are aware of the Lilly Endowment's ongoing support of religious life and religious studies. It is, by a long way, the largest funder of academic research about religion in America, including the research project from which this book is drawn.

What many do not realize, however, is that spending on religion represents only about 20 percent of the money dispersed by the Endowment. The Lilly Endowment spends much of its money on education throughout the state of Indiana, on matching grants to local county-based foundations, and on programs that benefit the Indianapolis community directly. In 2000, the Lilly Endowment made 34 percent of its grants—representing approximately $198 million—just in Indianapolis/Marion County.

Many smaller foundations and nonprofit organizations receive large portions of their budget from the Endowment. Start-up capital for the RCA Dome (home of the NFL's Colts), the amateur athletic complex that has recently drawn the National Collegiate Athletics Association (NCAA) headquarters to the city; the zoo; the downtown Artsgarden attached to the Circle Center Mall; and numerous other civic projects were undertaken with Endowment support. It is not possible to understand the world of congregations or social services, much less their connection to civic life, in Indianapolis without understanding something about the role played by the Lilly Endowment.

Moreover, people in Indianapolis *know* that the Endowment is crucial to community life. In a recent survey done by the Polis Center, more than 98 percent of respondents said that the Lilly Endowment was "very" or "somewhat" important to community development in Indianapolis, with 73 percent saying "very."

The many factors that create this social setting—relative homogeneity, little racial or ethnic friction, powerful philanthropic organizations, white majority control even of inner-city government—combine to create a specific context in which faith-based reforms might be undertaken.

## The Social Service Context

The role of the Lilly Endowment, along with other foundations, is especially important to the social service groups in the organizational ecology of Indianapolis. Proposed faith-based partnerships must ask themselves not only how their efforts will improve on or complement existing efforts but also what existing programs their new initiatives might harm or displace. In Indianapolis, they must ask themselves how the Endowment will view these partnerships and how existing funding streams might be altered for good or for bad.

Considerations of these sorts are important for a number of reasons. If nascent faith-based initiatives anger or alienate existing providers from the outset, they create a roadblock that may have been unnecessary. The point is not just that different organizations provide overlapping though different services, but that different people do the providing.

Juvenile court refers a finite number of cases to home-based counseling. Each case it refers to one of the new, faith-based providers means a case not referred to the secular social workers. In this instance, the new providers tended to be African-American, male pastors usually assigned to the families of African-American, juvenile males. The existing social workers are more likely to be white, middle-aged women, who had received bachelor's degrees or even held Masters of Social Work (MSW) diplomas.

There was, understandably, some tension at the outset. The social workers were suspicious of the pastors' credentials for the task at hand. They correctly thought of themselves as degreed professionals and would be hesitant to admit that religious leaders without formal training in social work (some pastors had such training, while others did not) could do the job as well. The pastors, for their part, wondered about the social workers' ability to serve young males in the African-American community. Obviously, there were unmet hopes and expectations, or the judge would not have experimented with new solutions.

It is easy to imagine that in any setting where faith-based providers will be displacing a professional bureaucracy, tensions will exist. The abstract notion that there is some large, impersonal welfare bureaucracy being supplemented by small, personalized religious communities evaporates at the point when the real people from each group must work side by side. Potential partners in any faith-based reforms—or any other welfare reforms, for that matter—must be prepared to deal with this inevitable tension.

There are other, pre-existing relationships to be considered. In every community, there is already a working coalition among government funders, philanthropic organizations, and the service community. Sometimes the balance is tenuous. In Indianapolis, for instance, there is always the question of how well the mayor's office works with the governor's office, and how well either of those organizations works with the Lilly Endowment. Relationships are fluid and subject to change through staff turnover as well as through elections.

There are already-existing relationships between servers, funders, and educational organizations. The servers work with the local primary and secondary schools in relationships that have taken considerable time and effort to build. On the other end of the educational spectrum, the colleges and universities are providing credentials for social workers and others in the service community. New religious partners change the equation, and they must consider carefully how their entry into the field affects existing arrangements (Hall 1997; Jeavons 1994; Benjamin 1997).

Finally, there are existing religious providers—Catholic Charities, Goodwill, YMCA, Jewish Federation, Salvation Army—who each already fill a specific niche in the service or community development markets. New faith-based partners must ask themselves how their efforts fit in with these. It is worth noting that in Indianapolis groups like Catholic Charities and the Jewish Federation are suspicious of new efforts that are explicitly sectarian, especially those that are congregationally based. At the same time, however, groups such as Goodwill are seeking to recover their religious roots in the interest of securing new resources in the changing environment of religious partnerships.

Obviously there is work enough to be done by everyone, since impoverished individuals and underdeveloped communities show no signs of disappearing. But faith-based reformers, however critical of current practices and partnerships, must acknowledge the good that is currently being done and seek to improve those efforts, or at least not to hinder them, even as they look for ways to improve services and development through their expanded participation (Millbank 1997; Orr 2000; Stone and Wood 1997).

## Religious Context

Few people ever stop to consider the importance of regional religious context, but nowhere are the weaknesses of the one-size-fits-all strategy more apparent. America has a broad religious mix, but the religious culture within regions varies tremendously.

For instance, on the northeast coast, in the Southwest, and along the southern California coast, more than half of the people who belong to any religious group are Catholic. Throughout the southeastern United States, however, Baptists of one type or another make up the largest single group in virtually every county. In the mountain states, and not only in Utah, there are as many Mormons as there are all other members of religious groups put together. In the Upper Midwest, there is a fairly even mix of Catholics and Lutherans, but all other groups are much smaller by comparison. There are large numbers of Jews from Boston to Washington, D.C., but especially in the areas of New York City, New Jersey, and the Washington, D.C. suburbs. In none of those places, though, are Jews the largest religious group. Elsewhere in America, with the exception of the Miami area, Jews are a relatively small minority.

Faith-based reforms must take account of these significant and often enormous differences in religious cultures. To establish a program in Providence, Rhode Island, for instance, one must work with the Catholic archdiocese because Rhode Island is the most religiously homogeneous state in the union after Utah. That is not to say that other groups are unimportant, but it is absolutely necessary to recognize the archdiocese's centrality and to realize that other groups are forced to define themselves over against that reality. Any competition that might arise, as well as any changes to the established service infrastructure, must account for relative size and strength among organizations.

The same would be true in Salt Lake City, except there the majority group is different. In Salt Lake City as in Providence, however, it would be possible to work with a central bureaucratic organization and to manage new partnerships through formal administrative channels. In a southern city dominated by Baptists, in which each congregation has a fair degree of autonomy, the same strategy would not work. It would be necessary to treat each smaller organization as a volunteer group and to work without central planning.

Indianapolis is an odd case because it has an unusually even mix of traditions. Catholics are the largest single group, but they represent only about a quarter of all church and synagogue members and only about 12 percent of the total population. Taken together, there are more mainline Protestants than Catholics. Similarly, there are more conservative evangelicals than Catholics if all the Baptist, Pentecostal, and independent groups are added together. This same sort of mix holds throughout the state. Indiana has a recognizably Protestant culture, but it is broken into a multitude of individual denominations and congregations.

Indianapolis is more Protestant than the Midwestern cities nearest to it. In Cincinnati, for example, Catholics make up half of the churchgoing population. In Chicago it is 65 percent; in St. Louis, 40 percent (Bradley et al. 1992). But in Indianapolis, Catholics make up only 23 percent of church membership. Only Columbus, Ohio (29 percent Catholic), has a religious makeup much like the one in Indianapolis. Interestingly, both cities were intentionally designed as state capitals because of their central location; neither evolved due to immigration tied to industrial economic opportunity.

From the beginning, Indianapolis was home to the major Protestant denominations now considered to be the "mainline." As Jan Shipps has pointed out, by the time Indianapolis was formed, the tradition of disestablishment was firmly rooted in the minds of Americans (see Bodenhamer 1994). Indianapolis was never, therefore, identified with a single religious tradition around which other communions orbited. It has had substantial numbers of Episcopalians, Lutherans, Methodists (black and white), Baptists, and Presbyterians for as long as it has been a city. It has had Christian Churches (Disciples of Christ) for as long as there have been Christian Churches. Indianapolis has historically had a religious core, but it is the multidenominational core of the American mainline.

By the mid-nineteenth century, Indianapolis also had ethnic Catholic parishes and a synagogue, as well as Black Baptist and African Methodist Episcopal (AME) churches; but it was clear that these groups existed alongside and around the Protestant establishment. As the mainline churches grew in power and as their national offices created the religious establishment that would dominate American life until the middle of the twentieth century, Indianapolis stood at the solid center of religious practice in the United States.

The mid-twentieth century saw gradual but steady changes in Indianapolis's religious landscape. Although the mainline denominations did not see any substantial membership declines, they also saw no growth as the city grew precipitously around them. There were as many Episcopalians and Methodists in Indianapolis in 1990 as there had been in 1950, but there were now twice as many people in the city. So by percentage, Episcopalians and Methodists were halved even as their real numbers remained constant.

The number of independent churches, especially independent Christian churches or Churches of Christ, continued to grow as did membership in these groups. At the same time, Indianapolis added many small, black Pentecostal and Baptist churches that are ubiquitous in cities across the nation. Although the Catholic population grew rapidly in the early part of the twentieth century, it too leveled off by the mid-1900s. Like the Protestants, Catholics did not decline but simply stopped growing. Indianapolis experienced relatively little Latino immigration compared to cities like Miami or Houston, so there was no influx of cultural Catholics into the city.

Similarly, Indianapolis experienced relatively little of the Asian immigration common to places like Detroit or Chicago, so it saw only small increases in the practice of Islam, Hinduism, or Buddhism. Even the opening of the Islamic Society of North America (ISNA) in 1983 in Plainfield, an Indianapolis suburb, did little to expand the Muslim population here. ISNA continues to be an administrative hub for certain Muslim interests in America, but the mosque serves a small population.

Indianapolis has had a small but steady Jewish population since the mid-nineteenth century. Today five synagogues serve roughly 6,000 regular members, and there are approximately 10,000 in the metropolitan area who identify themselves as Jews.

Indianapolis has, on the whole, a very diverse religious marketplace, especially if one follows the American tendency to treat Protestant denominations separately. Catholics are the largest religious presence in the city at 23 percent of religious adherents. However, once one factors in the reality that only about 50 percent of Indianapolis residents are church members, it becomes more accurate to say that Catholics make up about 10 to 12 percent of the population, compared to something closer to 40 percent in a city like Chicago.

The mainline Protestants together make up about one-fourth of religious membership and so outnumber Catholics slightly, although no single Protestant group is even half as big as the Catholic church in the city. United Methodists, at 10 percent of religious membership and roughly 5 percent of the total population, are the largest. The Christian Church (Disciples of Christ) continues to be an important factor in the community because both its national headquarters and a major seminary, Christian Theological Seminary, are located in Indianapolis. The rest of religious life is made up of independent Christians, Pentecostals, Black Baptists, Nazarenes, Missouri Synod Lutherans, Seventh Day Adventists, Jews, Friends, and an assortment of smaller groups, from both Western and non-Western traditions. Indianapolis has substantial numbers from many groups, each with a small but steady slice of the pie.

This is not to say, however, that Indianapolis therefore lacks a cultural core tied to religion. In fact, most of the city's business elite, including leadership at the Lilly Endowment, continues to come from the city's mainline Protestant establishment. The previous two-term mayor had Jewish roots, which may seem odd in a place where fewer than 1 percent are Jews, but the mayor before him was a Presbyterian pastor at one of the city's highest profile congregations. The chair of the Lilly Endowment is Presbyterian, as is the head of the religion division. The president of the Lilly Endowment is United Methodist. The city council member who spearheaded the move to Unigov is Presbyterian. The three congregations with the largest endowments, including Christ Church Cathedral on Monument Circle with $85 million, are all Episcopalian (as was Mr. Lilly, who funded all three of their endowments). The important pulpits in the tall-steeple white churches continue to belong, with only a few exceptions, to Methodists, Presbyterians, and Christians. Only recently has the prestige and social authority associated with these pulpits been challenged by pastors in the most important African-American congregations or the large independent community churches.

Indianapolis views itself as a town with little religious friction and is generally justified in thinking so. Whatever anti-Semitism individuals may harbor, there are few overt expressions of it. There are virtually no neighborhoods in Indianapolis where Jews would feel threatened because of their Jewishness. The Catholic archbishop makes few public pronouncements concerning moral issues such as abortion or capital punishment. Indeed, few of the leading clergy in Indianapolis could be described as activists on behalf of issues usually categorized as "social justice." Indianapolis is a city where religious life mirrors a mildly diverse, tolerant, and generally prosperous middle class.

Contemporary concern about religion's role both in building civil society and in delivering social welfare services must be understood within this particular urban context. Social action must be understood in terms of the many factors—history, race, class, polity, education—that surround it. Indianapolis is a particular place, to be sure, but so is every other place (Eiesland 2000; Livezey 2000). We develop a better understanding of the role religion does play and can play only when we understand how tightly it is intertwined with other social factors.

Throughout Indianapolis as throughout America, religion plays the dual roles of individual therapy and in-group community building. The business of most churches and synagogues is to equip members with the theological and ethical tools they need to make sense of their lives and to build a community capable of sustaining shared values through mutual support and encouragement.

No one should ever discount the valuable societal contribution that religious organizations make as they equip their membership in this way. A multitude of studies suggest that individuals who are embedded in religious communities are better adjusted psychologically, physically, and socially than their counterparts who are not embedded in such communities. At the very least, religious congregations teach moral values and provide networks of support. But they are also, in many cases, the places where individuals first learn to take leadership roles, speak in public, manage a budget, or follow Robert's Rules of Order (Ammerman et al. 1997).

Congregations are often criticized as "country clubs" that focus inward and turn all their attention to the care of their own spiritual needs, including the needs of their children and adolescents. Most reasonable people who have looked for very long at congregations, however, would say that this stereotype is usually not entirely true. Even to the degree that it is true, however, it bears mentioning that society may benefit from having constituents who are embedded in an inward-looking, member-serving "country clubs" that teach moral values—including the values of toleration and service to others—and that care for the moral and spiritual needs of children.

That said, it is undeniable that there is much current interest in the public role of congregations and religious nonprofits. It is these groups *as* groups, and not just their individual members, that are being asked to play a more important role in building the civic infrastructure. It is these groups as *organizations* that are being asked to help rebuild civil society and to provide social services, especially in inner city neighborhoods.

## A Context of Rising Expectations for Faith Communities

To say that congregations are being asked to accept this enhanced social responsibility is, on one hand, just a way of saying that hopes and expectations are changing. There is a vague but nonetheless real sense that society, on many levels, is moving away from governmental control of the welfare state toward an environment slanted much more heavily toward private organizations, including congregations and nonprofit service groups.

This ecology of religious organizations requires a genuinely multifaceted approach. Some efforts must aim for individual pastors and laypeople. Other efforts must still aim at the bureaucracy or at religious leadership of centrally managed organizations. There are very real differences not only in theology but also in race, social class, and ethnicity among these different groups.

Faith-based strategies may work in Providence, Salt Lake City, and Indianapolis, but the same strategy is unlikely to work in all three. Until faith-based partnerships are able to think critically about their own ecology of religious organizations and to see these in the context of the political and other service organizations, they are likely to create more detours and roadblocks than are necessary.

Not every organization that considers a new faith-based partnership, whether the mayor's office or a small congregation, can afford the time and effort required to consider every variable in the ecology they would serve. But they must give at least some thought to the political, social service, and religious environments they are entering. They must consider how the various pieces fit together. Most importantly, from an ecological view, they must consider how each organization gets its resources and how shifts in the ecology will filter out to many other organizations. The point is not that dynamic change is bad or that maintaining the status quo is always good. Elements change naturally in any ecology. But we know as human beings living in an all-too-fragile natural environment that our intervention sometimes has unintended consequences that are often problematic and occasionally disastrous.

Contextual, environmental factors are more important than welfare reformers have recognized to date; and the differences among regional, metropolitan, and local environments are greater than even social scientists have acknowledged. The fact that we are a mass-produced society has led us to the complacent view that one size will fit all. But if the proposed advantage of faith-based services is that they will provide local, values-based alternatives to an impersonal bureaucracy, then it is vitally important to recognize that one size assuredly does not fit all.

## Sharing the Assumptions

All of the faith-based reforms underway in Indianapolis operate in the same urban ecology. Moreover, each shares the assumptions common to new faith-based initiatives. The efforts of the mayor's Front Porch Alliance, especially, embody all three assumptions about values, subsidiarity, and locale. The mayor's intentions were unambiguous:

> We looked at how we could use media and the institutions, not-for-profits and faith-based, in order to look at building up communities from the inside out. We looked at this in three different ways. The first was how these neighborhood based organizations actually help develop social capital—like how they create connectedness in their communities. The second was how they are non-bureaucratic mechanisms to respond sensitively to people in the community. . . . And third, we looked at value enhancing activities. (Goldsmith 1998)

The mayor's approach to congregations and other faith-based groups was aggressive, as was the concurrent HUD approach at the national level. Although Mayor Goldsmith was explicit that congregations and religious groups could not do it all, he was equally clear that congregations and faith-based groups must bring their gifts to the table. And those gifts include not only religious values and nonbureaucratic flexibility but also the sense that they are "neighborhood based."

The juvenile court judge's office operated on similar assumptions. Judge Payne was clear from the beginning that he believed congregations offered values and ethical teaching that other organizations did not. Moreover, they represented moral communities from which he hoped juvenile delinquents and their families could draw strength and support. The judge's office was very clear that it was not requiring social work or counseling credentials. Indeed, Judge Payne felt that insistence on certain professional credentials raised the price and lowered the quality of services received by juveniles. He was, in a word, much more interested in *character* than in *technique*.

Although Judge Payne also assumed that congregations in the neighborhoods most afflicted by juvenile crime would be likely participants, location has never been a strict qualification. In that sense, his program was less neighborhood-based than the mayor's.

The CHIP initiative was undertaken less because of assumptions about locale and more because both the Endowment and CHIP believed congregations were under-utilized, under-informed actors in issues of homelessness. As with the other two efforts, the CHIP proposals were clear in describing congregations as partners. Neither local government nor the nonprofit sector were handing congregations the keys and telling them to turn off the lights when they finished. But congregations were, nonetheless, being asked to join in the world of grant writing as well as program administration and evaluation. They were being asked, gradually but surely, to learn about, and to consider participating in, the new social order created by welfare reform.

Civic leaders from nonprofit organizations and from government as well as religious leaders must keep these reforms in cultural and historical perspective. Given what else they know about the city, they must ask hard questions about what will work and why. A useful starting point is a closer look at congregations as a type of social organization. From there we can turn to further examination of the three assumptions—local knowledge, subsidiarity, and values transformation—that drive faith-based reforms, considering each in the light of a better understanding of the city's social and organizational ecology.

# 3  Types of Congregations

But whether congregations have worked for good or ill or both at the same time, they have been indispensable in shaping American society and the American character. It is our belief that awareness of their enormous impact on American life is beginning to dawn, promising for American congregations a more visible and valued place in our imaginations. (Wind and Lewis 1994)

The future of faith-based partnerships and of congregations as civic actors must be understood within the social context in which faith-based experiments will unfold, including some understanding of the broader social ecology that includes the prevailing political and organizational culture at the national, state, and local levels. But they must also be understood in the light of enormous, important differences among congregations as organizations. Those who advocate congregational involvement in welfare reform often paint social environments and religious organizations with too wide a brush. The ability of congregations to be effective partners in service provision hinges on the ability of other potential partners to differentiate meaningfully among types of congregations in their social environments.

While most people know a great deal about their own congregation, if they belong to one, few people know much about any other congregations. Consequently, most are unable to generalize meaningfully about congregations as a type of organization. Even very large differences among congregational types—such as the fact that Catholic parishes tend to be arranged geographically, while Protestant churches are usually not, or that inner-city neighborhood have many more, much smaller congregations per capita—are not part of public discourse.

One small example from Indianapolis highlights the importance of recognizing the variation among congregations. Ram Cnaan, Professor of Social Work at the University of Pennsylvania, conducted research on Indianapolis as part of his excellent study on behalf of Partners for Sacred Places. During his research, he did a detailed analysis of the services provided by twenty-five congregations housed in historic buildings. The average congregation in his study had 517 members. He looked at every form of community service they provided, including use of space for public meetings, volunteer help, and cash outlays. Cnaan concluded that on average the congregations he observed put $144,000 per year in cash and services into the local community. Of that, $33,000 was actual cash outlay built into the budget (Cnaan 1997).

*The Indianapolis Star* ran a story based on this research, claiming that the average congregation in Indianapolis spent $144,000 on the community. If this were true, the 1,200 congregations in Indianapolis were doing some $173 million dollars ($144,000 x 1,200) in public spending. There was, of course, no way such a large sum could be possible.

What was the difficulty? When the newspaper extrapolated from Cnaan's research, it made the mistake of generalizing to all congregations what had been found only about congregations housed in historic buildings. Those historic congregations, it turns out, were overwhelmingly more Catholic and mainline Protestant than congregations in general, so they were skewed toward groups with more members with a higher social class and greater income.

But the greater difficulty was much broader. Although Cnaan was careful to circumscribe his conclusions, the data led to public generalizations that were unfair and, to some degree, untrue. In the service world of model programs and best practices, people were pointing to the very few large, well-organized programs and saying, "This is a model." Sociologically speaking, those cases were anecdotal. The stories were true as far as they went, but they were not representative. Seriously atypical congregations in very specific social circumstances were being used to shape the activity of congregations that had very different circumstances. In a more insidious way, the raw numbers themselves were creating the same kind of problem. Clearly, people who were planning faith-based partnerships or were writing about the role of the faith community needed a greater awareness of variation among congregations. Several variables required much better explanation.

## Religious Traditions

The most obvious place to look at differences among congregations is religious tradition. Some congregations are Catholic, some are mainline Protestant, some are evangelical, some are Jewish, and so on. When most people think of these differences, they think of differences in theology: "Catholics believe this, but Methodists believe that." These theological differences are important, but there are organizational differences that must be understood as well.

One enormous difference is between Catholic congregations, which tend to be parish-based, and Protestant congregations, which generally are not. Since Vatican II Catholics have been less strict about residence and church membership, but in general Catholics are expected to attend the church that serves the neighborhood where they live. The churches have defined geographic boundaries that serve as catchment areas. Catholic parishes often have schools as well. In Indianapolis, where public education is still defined by forced busing for the purpose of desegregation, these parish schools are often the de facto local schools where many non-Catholic neighbors send their children. On the other side, although some Protestant congregations do recognize geographic responsibilities, few are organized into regions with clear, pronounced boundaries. Clearly, this difference in organization has everything to do with welfare reform, especially since local knowledge is one presumed benefit of such changes. But Catholics and Protestants are too often treated similarly.

Related to the Catholic/Protestant distinction is difference in polity. Some religious traditions organize themselves around an "episcopal" model. That is, they have bishops, with perhaps an archbishop presiding over them, and priests and other functionaries who all reside in a spiritual and managerial hierarchy. Different groups assign authority differently—indeed, even among Catholics or Episcopalians there are wide differences from place to place—but the general style of episcopal governance defines organizations such as the Roman Catholic communion, the Orthodox churches, Episcopalians, Lutherans, Methodists, and some Pentecostal traditions.

Other religious traditions are more clearly "congregational" in polity. Each congregation runs its own finances, maintains its own building, and calls and pays its own leaders. Frequently these groups operate cooperative programs for various missions, but in general each organization is autonomous. Baptists, Jewish synagogues, United Church of Christ, Disciples of Christ, Quakers (along with the other "peace churches"), Unitarians, and independent congregations all follow this model, as do some Pentecostals. In general, Presbyterians would fit here, though they are perhaps the most difficult organization to define along this axis.

Again, there is great variation in the degree of autonomy for each organization, and the centralization of cooperative money and power varies widely. Nonetheless, traditions with congregational polities are quite different from those with episcopal ones, and faith-based reformers ignore those differences at their own peril.

The discussion of religious cultures in Chapter 2 pointed out how leadership is handled differently and how each group must be approached with forethought. For instance, it is possible to work through the Catholic or Episcopal hierarchy but not so easy to do so with Baptists. But these are not the only important differences. Catholic and Episcopal parishes are not meant to be direct competitors with other parishes within their denominations because their catchment areas are bounded. Membership is more centrally managed and resources are, to greater and lesser degrees, spread according to principles of managerial efficiency. But Baptist congregations are frequently in competition. If they compete for available grant funds or if they form coalitions with competing neighborhood groups, they could exacerbate rather than mediate existing divisions.

Another important distinction among congregations from different theological traditions is the way leadership is exercised. In the more episcopal traditions, bishops or synods appoint priests or pastors to the congregations. In a sense, these people are chosen from a central pool and can, within certain limits, be reassigned at the bishop's or the synod's discretion. Very often priests or pastors in episcopal traditions are hired "for life," and their ongoing maintenance is the responsibility of the entire body, not just of one congregation. Groups with congregational polity, however, generally call their own pastors. The denomination may be involved in shared, cooperative retirement or insurance programs, but the contractual arrangement is between the individual being hired and the specific organization doing the hiring.

Differences such as these affect the way congregations pursue faith-based reforms, not least because it has everything to do with who pays the bills. Congregations that generate all their own funds and pay all their own expenses may be especially attracted to government or foundation programs that will pay them to conduct their ministry. A pastor with an interest in juvenile delinquents, for instance, might consider contracting with juvenile court to provide much the same counseling he was providing already for free, albeit under certain administrative requirements imposed by the court.

Another salient question about the role of religious leadership has to do with the clergy's community standing. Most ministers, by definition, occupy a place of some respect. But some pastors are recognized as political and civic leaders as well as spiritual ones. In poorer communities with less political and economic— that is to say, *institutional*—power, pastors often assume the role of political leader. This is especially true among African-American churches. Therefore, political and foundation leaders trying to build faith-based partnerships must think carefully about the many roles religious leaders may fill. If they assume that all pastors play the same public role as in whatever model of clergy they know best, they will be unhappily surprised.

## Congregational Size

Perhaps the least-appreciated fact in the movement to involve congregations in civic life is just how much congregations, as organizations, vary from one to the next. At some very basic level, they are similar. Most have worship services weekly or more frequently. Most employ at least a part-time pastor or have someone who is serving a shift as clerk. Most, though not all, have some sort of musical program related to their worship and some sort of arrangements for teaching their religious stories and values to their children.

Beyond these similarities, though, congregations vary enormously. And as the example cited above suggests, there is great danger in extrapolating from the experiences of a few congregations to draw meaningful conclusions about the whole. The most insidious problem involves using the work of a few very large, very atypical congregations as the example for others to follow. Too often faith-based welfare reforms are promoted by reference to some model program in a congregation that varies considerably from the norm.

Having observed more than four hundred congregations in seventeen neighborhoods of Indianapolis, we have found that the mean congregation has roughly 400 members. That is, if one added up all the congregational members in Indianapolis and divided by 1,200 congregations, one would find about 400 members per congregation. This is what most people mean by average. However, the median congregation—the one at the midpoint between the largest and smallest congregations placed in rank order—has closer to 150 members. Put another way, fully half of all congregations in Indianapolis have fewer than 150 members.

These distinctions are important for two reasons. First, a small number of very large congregations are propping up the average. Indeed, one must reach the 70th percentile before congregations have 400 members or more. This means that only 30 percent of congregations are at least as big as the "average."

We noted the same differences in congregational budgets. The mean congregation in our sample has an annual budget of roughly $260,000. But the median budget is only about $125,000. Fully half of all congregations have budgets below $125,000 annually. And only one in five have budgets exceeding $250,000. Again, only the top 20 percent are at least as big as the "average."

Other questions concerning congregational capacity followed suit. The mean number of full-time, paid staff at a congregation was 2.75. But the median number was, as one might expect, 1. The practical realities lying behind this statistic are telling. Fully 30 percent of congregations have only one full-time, paid staff member, but another 27 percent have none. Another 12 percent have two. This means that nearly 70 percent of congregations have zero, one, or two full-time staff members, yet the mean is 2.75. Again, a relatively small number of congregations with very large staffs are inflating the averages.

## Numbers, Numbers, Numbers . . .

Our research reveals that the top tier of congregations, something like the largest one-fourth or one-fifth, have a very large share of the members and control a very large share of the money. In some urban neighborhoods, the single largest congregation accounts for as much as 80 percent to 90 percent of all social service spending done by the congregations there. In the total sample, only 20 percent of congregations spend as much as the mean congregation spends on social services. When only one-fifth of a group is "average" or above, there is something wrong with what one means by average.

To calculate a mean, one would put all of the members and all of the money into one pot and then divide by the total number of congregations. Therefore, a mean represents a per capita or prorated share of the whole. It can be used as a comparative measure, but it can also be misleading. It is misleading, for instance, as a characterization of how a typical congregation is likely to look. To know what any given congregation chosen at random is likely to do, or what the majority of congregations are likely to do, some measure other than the average, taken as the mean, must be employed.

Of course, a host of other variables influence the definition of typical or average as well. We arranged our data by theological groupings and found, not surprisingly, that mainline Protestant churches are larger than either the mean or the median and that Catholic churches are much, much larger, generally nine or ten times as large as the median of all churches. Their budgets follow accordingly.

Our data suggests that everyone interested in congregations as organizations

—from civic leaders to readers of the morning paper—should ask hard questions about any information in which the majority of the congregations being discussed are Catholic or mainline Protestant. These data are not inherently wrong, but they cannot be used to generalize usefully about other congregations. In Indianapolis, for instance, only 300 of the 1,200 congregations are from the Catholic tradition or the Protestant mainline. These groups combined make up one-fourth of the congregations but have roughly half of all members.

The same problem can apply within evangelical or independent congregations. A few mega-churches with several thousand members can badly skew an "average" being used to describe the field as a whole. There is, in fact, good reason to ask whether mega-churches and Catholic parishes should be treated separately because the size of their memberships and budgets as well as the range of their programs so obviously slants any concept of "average."

## Why Is This Significant?

These questions about relative size and balance should help civic leaders, and indeed all of us interested in faith-based reforms, to think more constructively about the role congregations can play. The lesson is not, of course, that only big, rich groups can get anything done. Small congregations can and do have substantial impact. The lesson of means and medians in everyday interaction is caution in making sweeping generalizations or in recommending one-size-fits-all "model" programs.

When congregations think of themselves as organizations—perhaps when they are making strategic plans or evaluating their annual efforts—they should maintain a realistic frame of reference. Are they smaller than average? Do their members give more or less than the average? How do their community ministries stack up? Serious answers to all of these questions require narrowing the frame of reference so that the "average" used for comparison is meaningful.

It is tempting for congregations to say, "We should just be ourselves and not worry about how we compare to any other group." But no organization behaves in this fashion, nor could it. Any human activity conducted in the presence of others uses those others as a mirror by which their own actions are observed, evaluated, and modified. Most congregations do not want to be islands, cut off from connection to others. They want to relate to the world in ways that make sense both for themselves and for those they serve, and that involves the use of conversation and comparison. They want to be a contributing, interdependent part of the community ecology.

Like all organizations, congregations can use the available data to think critically about their activities. They need not use the limitations of data (and all data has limitations) as an excuse to say, "Well, that doesn't really apply to our case." But in their critical thinking, they must do the difficult contextual work of asking *how* the available information applies to them. Statistical data are general and therefore must be put into context. Contexts *are* specific, so the broadest generalizations seem often not to fit. But organizations, including congregations, benefit most when they can figure out what the generalized information tells them about their specific situation. The question is not so much How are we like or unlike the average? but What range of groups does that average include, and what does that information mean for us?

A lot of organizational research about congregations, led by the rise of consultants such as Loren Mead, formerly of the Alban Institute, has been about intracongregational practice conceived as a kind of business management. But a renewed emphasis on congregations as community-serving, community-building organizations calls for better research into congregations as types of organizations as well as research into congregations' roles in a complex community ecology. This means we must learn to ask better questions about differences in theological traditions, in the size of congregational memberships and budgets, and in the kinds of communities where they are located.

Even a cursory glance is instructive. The majority of congregations are smaller and have less money than early studies, shaped by statistical means and averages, would lead us to believe. Differences in denomination or theological tradition are strong predictors of capacity that have been insufficiently examined. The ongoing public discussion about religion's public role must be informed by a fair interpretation of the big picture. The question is not whether some congregations are capable of being effective partners in service delivery and community building than others or even whether that capacity might be built in congregations that do not have it currently. The answer to both of those is undoubtedly "yes." But that still leaves questions about the number or type of congregations under consideration. Meaningful public dialogue must begin with realistic expectations based on a fair accounting of the enormous breadth and variety among congregations as organizations (Byrd 1997; Boris and Printz 1997; Boris and Steuerle 1999).

## Social Context, Tradition, and Community

A congregation's history, its theological tradition, the ethnic or racial roots of its members—all of these factors and many more besides help to establish the role such a group might play in faith-based partnership. Perhaps the best example of these salient differences is the relationship of black and white religious communities to the new reforms (Chaves and Higgins 1992; Jackson et al. 1997).

Faith-based reform has a very different meaning for people of faith in the black and white communities in America, as does the concept of Christian community renewal. The question of the congregation's role in the community is experienced very differently not only by congregants themselves but also by their neighbors who might not be believers at all. For significant historical and cultural reasons, the role of black church in the African-American community is not the same role of the white church in its community (Trulear 2000; Franklin 1997).

It is not fashionable to draw hard racial distinctions because they cannot help but lead to overgeneralization. But in Indianapolis, as in most other cities, residence is still largely segregated by race, even if somewhat less so than was true in the middle of the twentieth century. Many African Americans still think of themselves as members of an ethnic community within the larger community. Everyone recognizes that there is a great diversity of opinion among African Americans and that virtually all African Americans consider themselves to be members of the broader American society too. But neither of those facts diminishes the claim that there is a recognizable "black community" in Indianapolis.

The role of religion in that community, and specifically the role of congregations as community-building organizations, is stronger than in the white community as a whole. This may sound obvious, given the historical exclusion of African Americans from other organizations in America and the large role of the church in the civil rights movement. It may also sound stereotypical, since it does not apply to every person or every organization with the same degree of accuracy. But as a generalization, it is nonetheless true.

A survey of Indianapolis residents showed just how wide the gap could be. At the risk of causing the reader's eyes to glaze over, here are some findings from that survey that help illuminate the differences. African-American respondents were 40 percent more likely than white respondents to describe themselves as "very religious or spiritual." In all, 52 percent of African Americans offered this self-description, while only 37 percent of whites did.

African Americans were more than twice as likely—63 percent compared to 30 percent—to say that the Bible was to be taken literally as the Word of God. They might well have heard this at church, because in the last week 64 percent of African Americans reported they had been to church one or more times, while this was true for only 47 percent of whites. And it was not just this particular week. Overall, 39 percent of African Americans reported attending church more than once a week over the past year, while only 13 percent of whites said the same.

When it comes to religious education or programs or lectures, 41 percent of African Americans said they attended once a week or more in the past year, compared to 16 percent of whites, a difference of roughly 250 percent. One might argue, as the devil's advocate, that African Americans simply find it more necessary to tell survey researchers that they attend worship regularly because that is normative behavior. But responses to other, more practical questions suggest that these distinctions are very real and not just a matter of polite conversation.

When asked whether religious beliefs are important in making financial decisions in secular life, 84 percent of African Americans said they were, compared to 52 percent for whites. When asked whether religious beliefs were important in political decision making, 77 percent of African Americans said that they were, compared to 65 percent for whites.

Tellingly, 97 percent of African Americans and 93 percent of whites saw religious beliefs as important in making *family* decisions, so this is not a simple matter of one group being more religious than the other across the board. African Americans *are* more religious on many measures, but this is not a difference just in degree but in type. Nearly half of whites who say that religion is important in family decisions do not say it is important in economic decisions. African Americans do not make the same institutional distinctions.

On questions concerning the role religion should play in influencing public policy, the responses followed this pattern. Of African Americans, 94 percent said religious groups should influence policy on ethnic and racial issues. Only 78 percent of whites, still a substantial number, said the same. Similarly, 84 percent of African Americans said religious groups should influence policy on the minimum wage. Only 55 percent of whites said the same.

On the most telling question of all, the differences followed suit. When asked whether religious groups should receive state or federal funding to extend existing social welfare programs or to start new ones, 75 percent of African Americans said "yes," while only 55 percent of whites did.

These straightforward descriptions are not the result of some statistical sleight of hand. Each supports the other and fits seamlessly with other historical and contemporary observations about the role of black churches. Historically, the black church has been the center of the African-American community. When racial segregation kept African Americans out of prominent roles in business or politics, the black church offered positions of prominent community leadership. These churches were indigenous; they were the sole locus of autonomy and self-determination (Lincoln and Mamiya 1990).

It is not surprising, then, that political leaders such as Martin Luther King, Jr., Jesse Jackson, and Andrew Young came up out of the churches, or that other religious leaders like Malcolm X, Rev. Louis Farrakhan, or Warith Muhammed are also seen as civic leaders. Today there are more African-American political and business leaders who are not also clergy than was true a few decades ago, but they are still likely to have well-known, clearly defined religious affiliations.

The substantial differences reported in our survey point out that the "privatization" of religion is not the same for everyone. Many sociologists have argued persuasively that religion has become domesticated in American society. Against the strongest forms of secularization theory, they argue that individuals continue to be profess personal religious beliefs and to belong to congregations. But there is considerable acknowledgement that religion is more concerned with individual psychological experience and intimate institutions such as the family or ethnic community and less with large institutions such as government or business.

This argument for privatization is persuasive insofar as it is about whites in America, but it is obviously less true about African Americans. One can argue, and not without merit, that the trends are still present and that African Americans will gradually find their religious experiences more privatized and their churches less involved in civic affairs. But for the present, there is a gulf between the experience of white and black churches that is at least as pervasive as the organizational and territorial differences among Protestants and Catholics.

## Practical Differences

The different attitudes and opinions that surfaced in our survey are mirrored in the practices we have observed in Indianapolis. The examples of Mayor Goldsmith's Front Porch Alliance, the juvenile court's experiment with faith-based counseling, and the Coalition for Homelessness Intervention and Prevention (CHIP)'s transitional housing experiment make the case nicely. Each of these groups sponsored open grant applications for funds, and the level of response to these is telling.

The juvenile court sponsored the first of these competitions, as recounted in Chapter 2. Judge Payne's office received twelve applications. Staff members from the mayor's Front Porch Alliance provided substantial editorial assistance on several of the proposals. The mayor's office clearly saw this as an early opportunity to involve congregations in community life and to use the "soft" resources of the office to spur the growth of the nongovernmental service sector.

The next competition came from Mayor Goldsmith's Front Porch Alliance (FPA). They sponsored summer program grants that attracted 105 applications. Of these, 35 were from secular community organizations and 70 were from faith-based groups. In some ways this program was most useful because it allowed direct comparison between religious organizations and traditional community organizations in the same application pool.

The CHIP competition was the last of these three and required by far the most sophistication. As described earlier, CHIP hired a program officer to help interested parties write applications for the planning grants and then to help the planning grant recipients write their full program grants. CHIP received 7 planning grant applications (Table 3.1).

The first reasonable question concerned which kind of faith-based groups were applying for these funds. Although the term "faith-based organization" is frequently used, there is seldom much clarity about whether this means specific congregations or other kinds of nonprofits or cooperative organizations with religious ties.

In Indianapolis, congregations are the organizational locus of faith-based social service activity. Of the 89 faith-based applications, 64—or 72 percent—came from individual congregations or from named programs housed entirely within single congregations.

Of those 64 applications from congregations, 44—or 69 percent—came from churches that are evangelical in orientation. To simplify our analysis in a sample this small, we lumped all congregations together under two headings that represent, on the broadest scale, theological liberals and conservatives. Under the heading "Evangelical" we included all Baptists, Pentecostals, independents, and denominations with a conservative theological stance. We called our other heading "Liberal," under which we included all mainline Protestant denominations, all Catholics, and the black Methodist traditions such as African Methodist Episcopal (AME), Christian Methodist Episcopal (CME), and African Method-

**Table 3.1**

| Competition | Applications Received |
|---|---|
| Juvenile Court | 12 |
| FPA Summer Grants (secular) | 35 |
| FPA Summer Grants (faith based) | 70 |
| CHIP | 7 |
| Total | 124 |

ist Episcopal Zion (AMEZ). We were well aware that some mainline Protestants, Catholics, and black Methodists are evangelical in their theology, but we believe that the distinction drawn here broadly mirrors institutional differences representing more liberal, church-like approaches and more conservative, sect-like approaches. It is worthwhile to note that none of the applications were from non-Christian groups. This is not too surprising in Indianapolis, a city dominated by Christian traditions.

The fact that more than two-thirds of the applicants are from evangelical groups is not surprising on its face. As many as three-quarters of the congregations in Indianapolis, representing about half of all religious adherents, fall under the "Evangelical" heading. But this preponderance of evangelicals could be surprising to some, given that such congregations are by definition less "institutional" in their approach and less likely to be tightly networked to secular groups. Indeed, many evangelicals choose not to involve themselves with government or other secular groups on principle.

Upon further investigation, we found that fully two-thirds of the applying congregations were from churches with predominantly African-American memberships and that this fact accounted for the involvement by evangelicals. African Americans make up about 20 percent of the population in Indianapolis. Black churches, which on average are smaller than white churches, account for about one-third of the congregations in the city. By either measure, though, black churches were disproportionately over-represented among the applicants to these programs. A full 75 percent of the applicants to the juvenile court were from African-American congregations or coalitions of black churches and pastors (Farnsley 2001a).

Fully half of the programs proposed by faith-based applicants were new endeavors. Many of the congregations looking to enter the social service arena were drawn there by the appearance of the opportunities represented by these applications. Half of the new applicants were black churches; 55 percent of programs proposed by African-American groups were new. Perhaps even more importantly, 57 percent of the new programs proposed by faith-based groups were proposed by black churches.

The finding that so many programs are new initiatives is important. Anyone who has observed the nascent coalitions among government, secular nonprofits,

**Table 3.2**

| Competition | # new programs | % new programs |
|---|---|---|
| Juvenile Court | 7 | 58% |
| FPA secular | 11 | 31% |
| FPA faith-based | 32 | 46% |
| CHIP | 5 | 71% |
| Total | 55 | 44% |

and faith-based organizations involved in service delivery knows that there are two different movements underfoot. On the one hand, secular groups are seeking to tap into existing faith-based programs and to create networks among various programs already engaged in similar services. Both the juvenile court and CHIP were happy to look for religious organizations already doing this sort of work with whom they might develop a formal relationship.

A second movement is trying to encourage religious organizations to begin involvement or to increase their level of activity. The Front Porch Alliance, by design, hoped to encourage more religious organizations to take an interest in community affairs. The FPA's primary intent was always to grease the skids for faith-based groups that were interested in getting involved.

Nearly half of the faith-based programs were being proposed in response to this competition. The FPA's attempts to engage congregations, or at least to point them in this direction, seemed to be bearing fruit. The percentage of new programs was higher in juvenile court and higher still for the CHIP program. In the case of juvenile court, some congregations already working with youth informally or ad hoc found an opportunity to institutionalize their efforts and get paid for it.

In the case of CHIP—where more than three-quarters of the applications represented new programs—the situation was clear. No congregations in Indianapolis had ever taken on transitional housing in a large, programmatic way. The CHIP applications representing existing programs came from traditional homelessness service groups that had added congregations as partners for purposes of this grant. Any congregation or coalition of congregations ready to take this large step were basing their willingness on their ability to secure $150,000, an amount larger than the average Indianapolis congregation's annual budget.

There can be no question that money earmarked for faith-based organizations is increasing the number of programs sponsored by religious groups. If one adds the programs that expanded as a result of these grants, the percentage of programs raises from 50 percent to 60 percent. Close to two-thirds of all programs proposed for these competitions are either new or expanded because of this availability of funds.

Furthermore, there is no question that black churches are leading the effort to use these funds both to expand existing ministries and to start new ones. These facts align neatly with the survey finding that African Americans are much more likely to believe that congregations should get public money for these purposes.

## Indigenous Community Control

These numbers suggest that that efforts to get congregations more involved in civic life, and especially the welfare reform efforts to enlist religious help, mean something very different in the black churches than they do in the white churches. An event during the course of our research made this point very clear.

As part of our ongoing efforts to engage in public dialogue about our research and thereby to add useful information about religion to the realm of public planning, I wrote a briefing paper that asked ten hard questions about faith-based welfare reform. The questions I raised in that paper were drawn from many of the issues that now underlie this book. It was not a research effort intended to document and then argue for the findings, but rather it was a suggestion of concerns and questions I thought the faith community and the secular civic community should be asking.

A draft of that paper was circulated to staff at the Lilly Endowment; the head of the Central Indiana Regional Citizens League; some think-tank executives; leaders in the mayor's office, CHIP, and the juvenile court; and to selected clergy of all races. We invited them together for a discussion of the issues and to get their responses to the ten questions.

A group of angry African-American pastors crashed the meeting and dominated the proceedings. They were angry that I was questioning their ability to manage funds or to write effective grant proposals. They were even more angry that I was funded by the Lilly Endowment to do this, whereas they had been unable to get funding from the Endowment for their own projects. (The Endowment does not fund specific projects in specific congregations.)

At first I was flabbergasted. I had not singled out African-American congregations, although, as described above, it was now clear that black churches were doing most of the applying for grant funds. I thought, naively, that I was only raising questions suggested by my data—questions I thought the civic community, especially, should consider when realigning programs in order to encourage participation by congregations.

But the pastors framed the issue much differently. They saw recent reforms as a chance, finally, to put funds earmarked for social services and development in the African-American community under the control of African-American organizations. Doubtless this was also a chance to enhance their own social and political power in the community, but it represented a watershed in how money was allocated and which organizations were considered legitimate (Farnsley 2001b).

Seen in this light, particular questions about subsidiarity lose some of their force, and the question of "local" gets framed much differently. If there were problems in grant writing or administration, these pastors argued, then they needed more overhead funds and help in those areas. But to criticize any weaknesses they had seemed a backhanded way of denying their local control over the resources.

This description of events is not the confession of some guilt-soaked liberal. I still believe I was right to point out real and potential problems, which is, after all, one goal of the present volume. From the point of view of funders, whether foundations or government, questions of capacity to apply for funds, administer programs, or evaluate work are real and important. Moreover, they are questions that can only be answered empirically, and no one is served by hiding behind existing problems in interracial understanding.

Nonetheless, this interchange pointed out to me a justification for the new reforms that went beyond subsidiarity, the transmission of values, or the virtues of geographic locale. To these pastors, this was not about local control as defined by geography, but about local control as defined by ethnic and cultural community. Because they saw their churches as primary institutions in that community, they thought it healthy that funds and new civic responsibilities devolve upon them. The problem, in their view, was that government and foundations were asking them to accept these responsibilities without providing the funds, including the overhead funds, with which to do it. My criticisms of their organizational weaknesses were, then, fuel on the fire, because I was criticizing them for not doing precisely what they were saying they needed the money to do.

The same set of issues extends to the needed evaluation of programs and their results. Both funders and congregations joining in partnerships must be unambiguous about the goals. Obviously, there are specific goals such as number of families served or number of counseling visits per family, but the larger goals are often left hanging.

In what way, the participants must ask, will this new, faith-based, partnership be an improvement on current efforts? Will it save money by decreasing the funds spent on management and administration? Will it allow helpers who live nearer the needy to provide assistance? Will it cause the teaching of moral or religious values to be tied to the delivery of services? Or will it allow appropriate ethnic or racial or some other form of control over resources meant to help in that particular community?

Whether programs ultimately succeed depends on which yardstick one is using to measure. And if it is the case, as I am arguing, that the civic planning community and the black churches are using different yardsticks, then it will be very difficult to say whether efforts are meeting expectations. It will also be difficult to criticize efforts perceived to be falling short.

### Congregational Variation as the Primary Ecological Variable

As all of the proposed partners in faith-based reforms consider the shape their activities will take, they must take into account relevant factors in the national, state, metropolitan, and neighborhood environments. They must see each of the partners—and especially congregations, the newest partners—as interlocking parts of an urban whole. They must start by seeing congregations one at a time, understanding their role in particular social ecologies.

The point is not that each congregation must be approached as though it sprung new from the earth. Some generalizations are certainly possible and probably helpful. But these must fall into specific, predictable categories that put some teeth into assertions or assumptions about what congregations can do.

Anyone who hears claims for congregations' involvement should ask immediately, What size organizations are we talking about? Of a neighborhood they might ask, What factors best characterize this urban ecology and how are they related? A similar line of questioning instantly arises over budgeting and staffing. Facts such as these are neither incidental nor anecdotal; they are central to the future of community partnerships.

But those harder, more statistical indicators are only part of the necessary information. Potential partners or other citizens interested in such partnerships should be drawn quickly to the theological traditions, and especially to the polity, of the groups involved. Do the congregations in question call their own leaders, or does some larger bureaucracy assign them? Does the group emphasize personal evangelism and individual soul-winning, or does it see the world in more corporate, interdependent terms? Beyond these are even more serious questions about race and ethnicity. Interested parties must ask not only about the race of congregational members, but about the metropolitan and local racial context in which those members act. Who do they see as their audience or as the beneficiaries of their mission activities?

As we turn now to the three broadest assumptions that legitimate the push for greater public/private partnerships involving religious congregations, we must always keep in mind the socioecological factors that create their urban context. We do well to begin by understanding the most crucial aspects of the enormous variation among the congregations, the proposed partners, themselves.

# 4 How Well Do Congregations Know Their Neighbors?

> To achieve these goals, Federal assistance must become more effective and more tailored to local needs. We must not only devolve Federal support to state and local governments where appropriate, but move support out to neighborhood-based caregivers. . . . Reforms must make the Federal Government a partner with faith-based and community organizations that are close to the needs of the people and trusted by those who hurt. (Bush 2001)

Having thought contextually about the social setting and the important differences among congregations, it is now time to turn to the three basic assumptions that drive rising expectations about faith-based welfare reform. First to be considered is the potent, albeit sometimes subtle assumption by the public that congregations are service organizations and that they bear a special responsibility for those who live near their houses of worship.

Some congregations surely have this sense of themselves. But whether or not congregations think of themselves in this way, others in the community have clearly come to think this *about* them. In a survey of the Indianapolis population, 52 percent of respondents said that "serving others" should be congregations' highest priority. Among those who were *not* members of congregations, 68 percent named service as what congregations should be doing most. Because this expectation of service is so widespread, and because it is so often linked to the local neighborhood environment in the language of welfare reform, we must use the best available environmental and contextual information to ask what congregations are really doing.

When civic leaders such as then-Mayor Goldsmith or Juvenile Court Judge Payne turned to congregations, they did so because they believed that these were neighborhood organizations with both knowledge of, and interest in, the well-being of their local surroundings. Put simply, congregations are expected to love their neighbors, and their neighbors are assumed to be the people who live around the church building or temple, *even if the members of the congregations are not local residents themselves.*

The assumption that congregations have a local focus cuts much deeper than civic or governmental programs meant to enlist congregational assistance. Many neighborhoods have ministerial alliances or some other kind of coalition arranged by geographical territory. Neighboring congregations frequently form partnerships to address specific local needs. The idea of a parish model of ministry has strong appeal to many Protestants as well as to Catholics for whom it has been the traditional form of religious organization.

Catholic parishes are, however, becoming less territorial in focus (McGreevey 1996; Linnan 1995). In Indianapolis, we know that the average Catholic parish can expect that about 60 percent of its members live within the official parish boundaries. By contrast, only about 40 percent of the members of an urban Protestant congregation live in the immediate neighborhood. We also know that the percentage of parish members who live within the formal parish boundaries has decreased during this century. This decrease in proximity is no doubt due in part to ease of transportation. People are simply capable of traveling greater distances to work, shop, or worship. But this change is also due to the increased tendency of Americans to view membership in worshipping communities as wholly elective. Moreover, some post–Vatican II doctrinal changes relaxed the strictness of Catholic boundaries.

Many Protestants choose their church based on a combination of factors they find appealing. Protestants who move from one city to another do not always feel compelled even to select a congregation within a particular denomination. Catholics may feel more constrained to remain Catholic, but they are less likely today to worship at the church that serves the parish where they live and more likely to worship at another congregation that corresponds more to their expectations based on theology, lifestyle, culture, or other factors.

Most inner-city Catholic parishes in Indianapolis, as elsewhere, exhibit a high degree of commitment to the overall well-being of all the residents of their parish, whether they are Catholic or not. The determination of Catholics to open parochial schools to non-Catholics in the neighborhood provides an excellent example of this commitment. Given the serious problems faced by inner-city public schools, the fact that Catholics reach out as they do to local children is enormously important. In some areas, where public schools have lost a neighborhood focus due to forced busing, Catholic schools have become the de facto neighborhood schools.

The larger Protestant churches that are centers of urban ministry also take a local, if not quite parish-based, focus (Bos 1993; Green 1996). Any congregation that gets in the business of urban ministry learns quickly that it cannot serve everyone. Given that reality, the normal course is for the congregation to serve those nearest the church building itself. It seems odd for a congregation to travel past the needy at its doorstep to serve some other population elsewhere, although this surely occurs in some instances.

The smaller Protestant congregations, whether black or white, mainline or evangelical, are unlikely to be engaged in ongoing, programmatic, urban ministry. If they are doing urban ministry, they are likely to be involved right outside their front doors. Their missions are determined more by immediate need than by theology or demographic study. These smaller urban congregations simply respond where response is called for. A good example of this tendency comes from congregations that have programs for youth other than the children of their members. Although few congregations—fewer than 10 percent—have such programs, those that do are overwhelmingly more likely to serve youth who live immediately around the church building. What is striking about this pattern is that it holds whether the members of the congregation live in the neighborhood or not.

Because of the parish model, and because many inner-city Protestant congregations serve the most proximate, immediate social needs, it has become common to assume that congregations are, by definition, neighborhood-based actors with a vested interest in their local environments. From this has grown the assumption that congregations are more "on the ground," that they know their neighbors and their particular local cultures better than other groups. As Mayor Goldsmith put it, "Congregations know the needs of mom."

But is this true? Do congregations have better information about local circumstance than other kinds of organizations do? Are congregations more tied to local culture and local needs than other groups? Do they have theological and social justice commitments that tie them more tightly to their local environment?

The short, obvious answer is that some congregations are more "local" than others. Some congregations are dedicated to their local neighborhoods as a mission field, while others are dedicated to minister to the urban poor regardless of neighborhood. To understand the role congregations play in their local communities, however, one needs to understand some basic facts and distinctions about the urban congregational landscape. As leaders from local government, foundations, or nonprofit service groups think about partnerships involving congregations, they would do well to keep such distinctions in mind. As congregations think about their commitment to ministry in the local environment, these distinctions pose questions they can ask themselves.

The first key distinction has to do with membership and residence. Perhaps because of the older parish model, many people hold the mistaken assumption that church members live around the church. Some minds conjure up the picture of families walking to church on a pleasant Sunday morning. In fact, fewer than half of the average congregation's members—43 percent is both the mean and the median—live in the neighborhood where their church building is located.

The issue can be approached from the other side as well. In four inner-city neighborhoods in Indianapolis, we asked residents whether they attended worship regularly and, if they did, whether their house of worship was in their neighborhood. While extremely high percentages of respondents reported regular attendance at worship, only 45 percent of those said that they attended in the same neighborhood where they lived.

The simple fact that congregational membership and residency are not linked as closely as some might suppose does not prove that congregations are therefore disconnected from their local environments. It does, however, offer a prima facie challenge to claims that congregations are more "on the ground," or more attuned to local culture and the needs of local residents. Some congregations are deeply rooted in the local culture, as are certain other organizations, but this is not a generalization that can be confidently made of congregations as a whole.

## The Catholic/Protestant Distinction

Catholics are the archetypical case, although they are atypical for Indianapolis. Just as the parish has boundaries within which members are more likely than not to live, so do the priests usually live in a rectory that is part of the congregation's property. The *local* is, once again, more inherent.

As city government and local nonprofit groups in Indianapolis began thinking about congregations as new partners in service delivery or urban development, few leaders from those secular organizations had considered even this most basic difference—Protestant or Catholic—among types of congregations. Civic leaders who hoped to forge partnerships had not considered how this simple ecclesiological distinction could shape their chances for success right from the start.

There are other significant differences among Protestant and Catholic groups related to the difference between parish models and those that are based on something other than geography. Catholics, for instance, have historically formed their own institutions rather than working through secular or ecumenical institutions. Catholics operate their own substantial relief and social welfare services. They have traditionally created their own hospitals. They spend their resources on their own parochial schools rather than on reforming public schools.

It appears somewhat paradoxical at first that Catholics would be the separatists. The history of the Catholic Church in Europe, in many countries, has been substantially and sometimes even literally coextensive with the state. But in the United States in general, and certainly in a Protestant city such as Indianapolis, Catholics have developed parallel, separate institutions. They may work cooperatively with the government—Catholic Charities is a good example—or with the public school system, as the parochial schools do, but they maintain their distinct identity and retain administrative control over their own resources.

This distinction among Protestants and Catholics is not subtle. To historians or sociologists of religion it seems commonplace. But it is the sort of distinction not usually considered by those from outside the religious sphere who are trying to build new cooperative arrangements with congregations, even when those arrangements depend on the assumption that congregations are *local* organizations.

## The Black Church in an African-American Neighborhood

Anyone who assumes that congregations have particular local knowledge must recognize these differences between Protestants and Catholics. But there are other important distinctions too, some of which can also be described by thinking about the relationship of residence to worship location. There is, at least among whites in Indianapolis, a mistaken assumption that because black churches tend to be in neighborhoods where the majority of the residents are black, the members of those churches live in that neighborhood. As anyone who has ever studied black churches knows, this tends not to be true.

In Indianapolis, in fact, members of black churches are less likely to live in the same neighborhood as their church building. Of the congregations we visited, 86 percent had memberships substantially—90 percent of the members or more—of one race. For the average white congregations, 47 percent of the members lived in the same neighborhood as the house of worship, a percentage just slightly higher than the 43 percent that characterized the entire sample. For the average black congregation, only 36 percent of members lived in the neighborhood.

The combined facts that most Catholics in Indianapolis are white and that Catholics are more likely to live near their church undoubtedly contribute to this discrepancy. But the fact remains that black churches cannot be described as "neighborhood churches" simply because they are located in neighborhoods where the residents are black.

The empirical fact that African Americans also drive rather than walk to church does not, however, mean that black churches are not local organizations. But "local" assumes a somewhat different, less geographical meaning in this sense. African Americans are very likely to describe the congregations in their neighborhoods as important parts of the community. Residents may be frustrated when the congregations are not always engaged in ways the residents would prefer, but most, especially in poorer neighborhoods, see congregations as a net benefit.

This different sense of local in African-American neighborhoods, to which we will return, points out the difficulty in determining just what *local* means. Considering the proximity of members to their worship sites is a very empirical, objective indicator of the degree to which congregations are local organizations, but it is only one such indicator. There are other indicators of local involvement, some of which are subtle. Those who operate on the assumption that congregations have a local mission focus should consider these sorts of indicators too. Congregations benefit from asking themselves these same sorts of questions. The following categories all play a part in determining the "local" connection of congregations.

## Self-Perception

One way to think of congregations as local organizations is to consider their self-perception. Even if their members live elsewhere, do congregations, as organizations, concern themselves with the local neighborhood? Do they imagine that they have a special obligation to the people around them? If they have a mission statement (and many do not), does it outline the geographic nature of their intentions?

Given the geographic nature of parishes discussed above, Catholic congregations tend to have a local self-perception even if many of their members live beyond the established parish boundaries. Both parochial schools and local social services, such as St. Vincent de Paul societies, emphasize the responsibility of the congregation for the entire neighborhood.

Certain Protestant congregations also think of themselves as local actors even though they know that their members live elsewhere. Some mainline Protestant and black congregations revolve around a commitment to urban ministry. In many instances, these congregations have remained in neighborhoods where their now-suburban members once lived.

The phenomenon of urban ministry undertaken by nonresidents is complex. These urban ministry centers are undoubtedly able to bring needed resources into poor neighborhoods. The nonresident members of these congregations have, virtually by definition, more money and more connections to social power than do the poor residents of the neighborhood (Green 1996).

In many denominations the urban ministry congregations receive direct support from others for their mission activities. Both Catholics and Methodists, with their episcopal polities, are able essentially to tax better-off congregations and move the money into a variety of mission activities, including urban ministry. But even when the denominational structure does not coordinate this activity itself, individual congregations outside the inner city sometimes adopt urban ministry centers and provide material support.

Some congregations, therefore, attempt both to nurture a self-perception as "local" and to project that perception to a wider audience. In the broader religious marketplace, some consumers are searching for congregations that are doing urban ministry so that they can join or provide financial assistance. Certain suburbanites find urban congregations appealing for multiple reasons. Some choose to involve themselves in social justice issues. Some see urban congregations as more heterogeneous and cosmopolitan. What must be noted about self-perception is that it can change. To some degree, that perception of urbanity is elective, especially when it is not bolstered by empirical facts concerning where members live, shop, or work. And like any elective identity, this one is subject to revision.

## Historical Commitment

Sometimes congregations are considered integral to a local environment simply because they occupy such a longstanding place in the neighborhood's history. Congregations may be oriented toward the local neighborhood because their members once lived in that neighborhood, even if that connection is now several generations removed. Knowing how long a congregation has been in a place is a helpful clue in determining local commitment.

On average, congregations in Indianapolis have been in their present neighborhood for forty-seven years. In the inner city, the average is closer to fifty years. Those fifty years represent two very different countervailing trends in urban congregational life. On the one hand, many of the congregations in what might be called the downtown, or the inner city, have very long histories that predate the suburbs. On the other hand, a number of urban congregations have closed or relocated to areas far from the city center. As they left, new congregations arose related to new residents moving in.

Congregations may also have a historic commitment to a place because of their investment in their worship buildings or other facilities. The degree to which a congregation views its facilities as an extension of itself and the degree to which it sees that building as a vital part of the neighborhood landscape are important indicators. If other congregational programs—such as schools or daycare programs—are viewed as resources for the neighborhood that do not benefit only members, that would also imply some ongoing historical role within the neighborhood.

As both Secretary Cisneros and President Bush have done, it is common to speak of churches or synagogues as anchors in their neighborhood—but what does that really mean? Granted, the congregation may have been present longer than any other organization, but does it remain tied in meaningful ways to the residents or the other organizations in its ecology? Are members neighborhood residents, or were they once residents?

More than one respondent has suggested that congregations, by their sheer existence, provide a moral presence in a distressed neighborhood. That sentiment is usually expressed as, "If you think this place is bad now, imagine what it would look like without the churches." Others have suggested that congregations, if they are architecturally appealing, lend a cachet to the neighborhood that suggests hope and beauty. Both of these suggestions may be true, but those who are thinking critically about congregations must ask how strong a bond can exist if a congregation is connected to its local environment primarily by historical ties that have changed through the years.

## Neighborhood Networks

An excellent measure of a congregation's local involvement is the interaction the organization or its members have with other local actors, whether individuals or organizations. It is easy enough to describe and even to measure the networks the congregation as an organization has to other organizations in the neighborhood. It is more difficult, though ultimately more important, to discern the connections the members may have as individuals to that environment.

Some congregations work with other congregations in their area to address social-service needs or to create venues for socializing and recreation. Some groups work closely with neighborhood associations, community development corporations, economic development corporations, or neighborhood leaders.

When this happens, the congregation clearly views itself as a civic actor, as an organization with responsibility beyond the spiritual care of its own members and even beyond local evangelism. This is different from the "self-perception" mentioned above, however, because a congregation could see itself as local but have little interest in the sorts of cooperative efforts that are frequently civic and secular. Some Indianapolis congregations assume responsibility for a neighborhood's spiritual care and moral education but have little interest in neighborhood associations or housing rehabilitation. Some evangelical groups might witness frequently to those who live around the church building but do not promote economic development.

There are many networks, beyond obvious religious ties to denominations or other congregations, within which congregations operate: neighborhood interest groups, nonprofit social services, recreational services, and city or local government, to name a few. The degree to which a congregation participates actively in these other networks is one way to identify its commitment to the local community.

More crucial yet more difficult to describe accurately are the linkages that individual members within a congregation have either to organizations or to individuals in the neighborhood. Congregations must ask of themselves, and others should ask of them, whether they have open lines of communication within the local neighborhood. The point, once again, is not that congregations must have these things; each congregation can decide for itself both whether they have strong networks or whether they need to have them. The point is that if congregations are presumed to be assets as partners because they are local, then it makes sense to consider the *strength* of their local networks.

## Social Service

Most congregations provide some sort of emergency social services, at least to their members and their families. Many congregations provide services on a wider scale. It makes sense to ask how much of that service provision is aimed directly at the local neighbors. If congregations have food and clothing pantries for those who live around them, then that is a sign of local commitment and involvement. If their school, daycare facility, or other service provision is meant primarily to serve a local clientele beyond their own membership, that is another indicator.

One way to pose this question is to ask whether the congregation views social services to nonmembers as part of its mission. How much of its budget goes toward such services? Are staff members or volunteers organized to provide services in an ongoing, regular fashion?

In truth, the amount of social services provided by congregations to their local neighborhoods is very haphazard. We found that in a typical neighborhood, the average congregation spent about $19,000 on social services, a substantial sum, despite how small it might appear given the magnitude of the need.

But even that $19,000 figure should be regarded with caution. If one removes only the single largest-spending congregation from each neighborhood, the average drops down to between $1,000 and $3,000. So a handful of large congregations—typically Catholic parishes or very large Protestant churches with pronounced commitment to urban ministry—carry virtually all of the weight.

The degree to which evangelism efforts target the neighborhood near the worship building is a related indicator. If a group sees its primary mission as saving souls or creating new members from among the local neighbors, that is another way to think critically about local focus.

## Local, Public Space

Another way to think of congregations as local organizations is to ask to what degree they provide public space. In Indianapolis, at least, there are relatively few public meeting halls where neighborhood associations or Boy Scouts or Alcoholics Anonymous might meet. Congregations donate much of that space (Cnaan 1997).

While public space is undoubtedly a public benefit and congregations enrich their communities by providing it, it may or may not create a strong link between the organization and its neighbors. In some cases, the use of the space is anonymous. It goes on when the members are not present, so no contact is ever created—or, in some cases, it is scrupulously avoided. In other cases, the use of space is contentious within the congregation itself. There are examples of basketball courts being opened to neighborhood children or meals and social activities being catered for the elderly only to be quickly cancelled because a population that the congregation found threatening began to take advantage of these opportunities.

The provision of public space by congregations makes them important local organizations, but it does not, in and of itself, create social capital or deepen social ties. So while it is important to see this space as the important contribution that it is, it is also important to recognize what it is not.

## The Connections Between Congregations and Their Neighborhoods

There are certain transparent connections between congregations and the neighborhoods where their worship sites are housed. Small storefront black churches do not appear suddenly in edge cities. Large white community churches do not build many new buildings in the core of the inner city. No generalization is without exception, but as a rule there is congruence between types of congregations and the places where they are located.

Given that congruence, it is reasonable to assume some cultural assonance between congregations and those who live near their houses of worship. One might expect common social class, common worldviews, and something of a common use of language. Given the other specific connections that some congregations have by virtue of their history in, or service to, a place, it is also clear that some congregations have deep ties to their places and to their neighbors. But insofar as recent discussions about the role of congregations in social service delivery or community development have assumed that *most* congregations share these deep ties with their neighbors or that they have valuable, specific local knowledge, they have erred.

In the pilot stage of our project, high-school students conducted oral history interviews and looked for broad generalizations about religion and community. They focused their attention on four inner-city neighborhoods. Two of these neighborhoods, Mapleton-Fall Creek and Martindale-Brightwood, became the archetypes for thinking about religion's role in building a civic social environment (Farnsley 2000b).

Although both of these neighborhoods were mostly poor and mostly black and thus fell under the rubric of "inner city," the students noted significant differences between them. Mapleton-Fall Creek seemed to have stronger community programs revolving around health care, housing development, and social welfare services. Moreover, the faith community, especially the congregations, seemed integrally involved in these programs.

Although the students were not able to delve critically into the differences between these neighborhoods, they had correctly noted a variation in neighborhood environments that required explanation. As the project developed into a more traditional research effort, one of the early goals was to uncover and explain the variation in religious activity in its neighborhood context. What we began to find was that local nuance matters, because the kinds of organizations and the patterns of practice in urban ecologies—even cut as finely as individual neighborhoods—vary according to features such as ethnicity, economic base, and regional religious tradition.

There is a bias in public policy toward interpreting the reality of a situation through analysis of contemporary demographics. That bias suggests that if one knew the numbers up to the minute—race, family size, income—then one could shape policy accordingly. Our research on urban Indianapolis suggests this approach has significant limitations, especially when applied to the role played by congregations. The historical and social features that shape a neighborhood are not incidental, or even merely interesting, to a critical understanding of the role congregations play in a given place. Congregations fill specific niches in contemporary urban ecologies, and we cannot understand that niche unless we already understand the key features that have shaped the ecology.

A little closer look at Martindale-Brightwood and Mapleton-Fall Creek helps to illustrate the importance of local variation and the contributions of historical study to current policy. By contemporary demographic measure, these two neighborhoods are quite similar (Table 4.1). If the inner city were considered very broadly, as it often is, then one would expect that the congregations in these neighborhoods played similar roles in the local ecology. One would expect that the sort of community building they do and the kinds of services they deliver would be much the same.

In fact, the community-building and social service delivery efforts of the congregations in these neighborhoods are quite different. This is so, not because

**Table 4.1. Contemporary Demographic Comparison of Mapleton-Fall Creek and Martindale-Brightwood Neighborhoods**

|  | Martindale-Brightwood | Mapleton-Fall Creek |
|---|---|---|
| Population | 11,289 | 16,167 |
| % black | 95 | 88 |
| %senior (>65 yrs) | 13 | 14 |
| % youth (<19 yrs) | 35 | 31 |
| % HS graduates | 51 | 60 |
| % college graduates | 5 | 10 |
| % single mothers | 47 | 53 |
| median family income | $14,975 | $14,135 |
| % below poverty | 38 | 33 |
| % vacant housing | 21 | 16 |
| % owner-occupied housing | 43 | 26 |

*Source:* 1990 U.S. Census.

the needs of the neighbors are so different—the needs are roughly similar, as the demographics would suggest—but because the congregations that make up the neighborhoods have little in common.

Mapleton-Fall Creek, the more populous of the two neighborhoods, has 19 churches within it. Martindale-Brightwood, smaller by a third, has roughly 85 churches, although the exact count varies annually. The average church membership in Mapleton-Fall Creek is over 500. In Martindale-Brightwood it is roughly 90. Half the churches in Mapleton-Fall Creek, and all but one of the large ones, have predominantly white members. Virtually all of the churches in Martindale-Brightwood have black members.

These details demand that we treat these two neighborhoods differently if we hope to understand the role religious organizations play in the social ecology of each neighborhood. But the differences cannot be explained by appeal to sociodemographic characteristics alone. In fact sociodemographics, as Table 4.1 illustrates, do not explain the differences at all. These two similar-looking neighborhoods have different religious ecologies because they have very different histories. The differences among congregations follow directly from the neighborhoods' different origins and, given those origins, different responses to the same watershed event.

### Mapleton-Fall Creek

In the first two decades of this century, the Mapleton area, as it was then known, developed as an early suburb. Seven bridges across Fall Creek were built between 1900 and 1911, linking the city to the downtown. The 1923 Zoning Ordinance made sure that the area would not be industrialized. It was a desirable place to live.

Mapleton-Fall Creek's prosperous residents built some of the city's finest

**Table 4.2. Mapleton-Fall Creek Racial Composition from 1930 Forward**

|         | 1930 | 1940 | 1950 | 1960 | 1970 | 1980 | 1990 |
|---------|------|------|------|------|------|------|------|
| % black | 11   | 14   | 18   | 38   | 79   | 88*  | 88   |
| % white | 89   | 86   | 82   | 62   | 21   | 11   | 11   |

*1980 and 1990 do not total 100% because of presence of other racial groups or "foreign-born" respondents.
*Source:* 1990 U.S. Census.


churches. Several of the Gothic limestone buildings still have a cathedral-like effect. They continue to house the mainline Protestant denominations that made up the city's cultural core at the time: United Methodist, Presbyterian, Lutheran, and Episcopalian. The city's then-premier high school, Shortridge, with alumni like Senator Richard Lugar and author Kurt Vonnegut, was located in this virtually all-white neighborhood.

No social arrangement lasts forever, but in the early part of this century, urban arrangements did not last long at all. Already by 1930 some of the neighborhoods even farther north along Meridian Street were becoming more prestigious addresses. Only a trickle at first, middle-class whites and blacks began to move into Mapleton-Fall Creek as wealthier residents headed north.

In 1950, state law required Indianapolis to integrate Shortridge High School, and the trickle turned into a stream. By 1960 white attendance at Shortridge was 72 percent. When court-ordered desegregation for the entire city was ordered in 1970, the movement of whites from the neighborhood turned into a flood. In 1930 the neighborhood was 90 percent white and 10 percent black. In 1960 that was 62 percent and 38 percent. By 1970 it was 21 percent and 79 percent. By 1990 it was 10 percent and 90 percent, a complete reversal in 60 years (Table 4.2).

Racial change was not the only major shift in local demographics. The population of the neighborhood was 25,000 in 1930. It was 25,000 in 1960, even after the early stages of integration. But by 1990 it had dropped to 16,000, losing a third of its population in three decades.

The rest of the story follows predictably. Real-dollar income was well above the Indianapolis average at the beginning of the century, and it was still 112 percent of the city average as late as 1950. By 1970 it was 70 percent of the Indianapolis average, with 15 percent of neighborhood residents living in poverty. By 1990 income was 49 percent—less than half—of the Indianapolis average, and one-third of the people in the neighborhood lived in poverty. Housing vacancies went from 1 percent to 15 percent in this time (Table 4.3).

### Martindale-Brightwood

Martindale-Brightwood is a recognizable Indianapolis neighborhood today, but as the name suggests, it developed as two distinct neighborhoods. In this case, the neighborhoods were very distinct—one white and one black.

**Table 4.3. Mapleton-Fall Creek Vital Statistics From 1930 Forward**

|  | 1930 | 1940 | 1950 | 1960 | 1970 | 1980 | 1990 |
|---|---|---|---|---|---|---|---|
| Population | 25,376 | 25,298 | 25,584 | 25,055 | 23,043 | 19,097 | 16,167 |
| % of Indianapolis median income | NR | NR | 112 | 95 | 70 | 61 | 49 |
| % below poverty | NR | NR | NR | NR | 15 | 22 | 33 |
| % vacant houses | 1 | 7 | 3 | 5 | 9 | 12 | 16 |

*Source:* U.S. Census.

The presence of both races extends back beyond the turn of the twentieth century. These were industrial neighborhoods at the center of a railroad hub. Martindale was home to many African Americans as well as to first-generation immigrants before 1900. Brightwood, a planned factory community, was home to skilled and unskilled white workers, many of whom were also recent immigrants.

Both groups built the kinds of churches usually found in such neighborhoods. Some of the oldest black churches in the city still line the main boulevard, now named for local civil-rights-activist Andrew J. Brown, in what was once Martindale. Brightwood had a mixture of Catholic, mainline Protestant, and independent churches.

Like Mapleton-Fall Creek, Martindale-Brightwood maintained some stability in the first half of the twentieth century. In the 1930 census, the combined neighborhoods had 22,000 residents. The white to black ratio was 60 to 40. In 1960 Martindale-Brightwood had 25,000 residents—almost exactly the same as Mapleton-Fall Creek for that year. The ratio by then had become 55 black to 45 white. By 1990 the black to white ratio was 98 to 2, and the population had dropped by more than half, from 25,000 to just over 11,000 (Table 4.4).

**Table 4.4. Martindale-Brightwood Racial Composition from 1930 Forward**

|  | 1930 | 1940 | 1950 | 1960 | 1970 | 1980 | 1990 |
|---|---|---|---|---|---|---|---|
| % black | 42 | 43 | 50 | 55 | 77 | 95 | 96 |
| % white | 58 | 57 | 50 | 45 | 23 | 5 | 4 |

*Source:* 1990 U.S. Census.

Other demographic features followed suit. Income dropped from 86 percent of the Indianapolis average in 1950 to 53 percent of the Indianapolis average in 1990. Unlike Mapleton-Fall Creek, Martindale-Brightwood was accustomed to being below the city average. But by 1990 it was simply poor. Poverty numbers were not reported in the 1930 census, but we can estimate from an income level at 86 percent of the city's that most people were hovering just below middle-class. By 1979, 20 percent of the neighborhood lived in poverty. By 1990, 37 percent did. Housing vacancies fell from 3 percent in 1930 to 21 percent by 1990 (Table 4.5).

**Table 4.5. Martindale-Brightwood Vital Statistics from 1930 Forward**

|  | 1930 | 1940 | 1950 | 1960 | 1970 | 1980 | 1990 |
|---|---|---|---|---|---|---|---|
| Population | 21,869 | 22,947 | 25,418 | 25,702 | 18,928 | 15,366 | 11,289 |
| % of Indianapolis median income | NR | NR | 83 | 76 | 69 | 63 | 51 |
| % below poverty | NR | NR | NR | NR | 20 | 28 | 38 |
| % vacant houses | 3 | 2 | 2 | 7 | 12 | 15 | 21 |

*Source:* U.S. Census.

The whites who had lived in Brightwood poured outward toward the suburbs from 1960 forward. But unlike the whites in Mapleton-Fall Creek, they took their churches with them. Hillside Christian Church, Brightwood Methodist, and Brightwood Church of Christ all relocated to the suburbs. St. Paul's United Methodist and St. Francis de Sales Catholic Church both dissolved in the 1980s. The Methodist and Catholic churches of Martindale remained, committing themselves to what was by then known as "urban ministry" (Diamond 1997).

### Similarity and Difference

In many ways, the story of Martindale-Brightwood ends much the same as the story of Mapleton-Fall Creek: richer, whiter people are gone; poorer, blacker people are present. But the role of congregations in the two neighborhoods is strikingly different. And that difference is best explained, not by where the neighborhoods ended up, but by where they began. The white working-class residents of Brightwood were quicker to abandon their churches and to relocate their spiritual loyalties. Eventually, many of the buildings they once occupied became black churches. The white churches of Mapleton-Fall Creek, on the other hand, have remained white. They have remained upper-middle-class and mainline Protestant.

How are these differences best interpreted? One must begin by thinking about why the neighborhoods formed in the first place. Mapleton-Fall Creek was a haven for relatively wealthy suburbanites. Martindale and Brightwood were worker enclaves.

Political geography played a related role. Mapleton-Fall Creek churches are strategically located on or near Meridian Street, the main corridor of Indianapolis. That is an important location. The Indianapolis Children's Museum and Lilly Endowment, Inc. are located on Meridian Street in this neighborhood, so these churches have a certain metropolitan "cathedral" feel that belies the current poverty of their neighborhood. Even if their pastors do not always feel like they are part of the civic and social power associated with Meridian Street, the rest of the city perceives them in this way. By contrast, the churches of Martindale-Brightwood are invisible to most of the city. An interstate highway cuts through the neighborhood, but the main surface streets are not highly traveled by nonresidents.

The watershed events in the neighborhoods were the same: white flight to the suburbs related to black in-migration and to eventual school desegregation policies. The demographic changes that followed the event look similar too. But the effect of the changes on local congregations was very different because the congregations themselves were different. The stories of white flight and current demography, even taken together, do not explain the difference among congregations. One must also know what the neighborhood was like before the change.

### Why Religious Ecology Matters

These differences in congregational ecologies matter considerably. The churches of Mapleton-Fall Creek have become well known for their social services to those who live around their buildings. Former HUD secretary Henry Cisneros praised an alliance of those churches, the Mid-North Church Council, as a model of urban ministry (Cisneros 1996).

But what is it a model of? Could the churches of Martindale-Brightwood, which are smaller and poorer, be asked to do the same thing? Or should the neighborhood be told: What you really need are some large, mainline churches with suburban members and plenty of money.

On the other hand, there is good reason to believe that community building within the neighborhood, the development of communication and trust that is sometimes called "social capital," is more likely to go on among the churches of Martindale-Brightwood. In a survey conducted in the two neighborhoods, respondents were asked to name the key people they turned to for support and guidance. For Martindale-Brightwood residents, those key support people are much more likely to live in the neighborhood and to attend the same church as the respondent than is true in Mapleton-Fall Creek.

The residents of Martindale-Brightwood are, as a whole, much more likely to attend worship in their neighborhood than are the residents of Mapleton-Fall Creek, although the percentage of residents who reported attending worship were roughly the same: 78 percent of the residents in Martindale-Brightwood and 76 percent of the residents in Mapleton-Fall Creek. But 55 percent of Martindale-Brightwood residents reported that they attended worship in their neighborhood, whereas only 29 percent of Mapleton-Fall Creek residents attended worship in their neighborhood (Table 4.6).

Therein lies a conundrum. In recounting these neighborhood histories, there is a bias toward explaining where the *white* residents of the neighborhoods went. If the story is about material resources that congregations provide to their neighborhoods, then there are good reasons to tell the story in just that way. The mainline and Catholic churches of the white middle class are, on balance, the custodians of greater financial resources. They provide social services and are able to bring both money and institutional connections from the richer

**Table 4.6. Average Size and Composition of Neighborhood Residents' Social Networks**

| | Mapleton-Fall Creek | Martindale-Brightwood |
|---|---|---|
| % of persons who report having a regular place of worship | 75.7 | 78.3 |
| % of persons who say their regular place of worship is in the neighborhood where they live | 28.9 | 55.1 |
| Number of persons in the respondents | 19.8 | 17.2 |
| % of persons in network who live in same neighborhood as respondent | 24.8 | 34.8 |
| % of persons in network who attend same congregation as respondent | 30.7 | 41.2 |

*Source:* Neighborhood survey conducted by The Polis Center, 1997, Arthur Farnsley and Eric Wright. N = 600 randomly selected residents, 150 from each of four neighborhoods.

neighborhoods where they live into the poorer neighborhoods where they worship.

Moreover, congregational size, independent of race, is a compelling variable when considering a congregation's ability to provide services or spur development. On a series of variables such as number of members, weekly attendance, annual budget, or spending done in the local neighborhood, we have consistently found that the *mean,* when all congregations in our sample are taken together, is more than twice the median. What this suggests is that congregations in the upper half on any of these variables are carrying a disproportionately large share of the load. In inner-city neighborhoods as much as 80 percent of the service and development work is being done by roughly 10 percent of the congregations. The story of material resources is a story of the relationship among variables such as race, economic class, theological tradition, and size of the congregations involved.

But if the story were told from the point of view of community building and networks of communication and trust, then it might sound very different. Although then-Secretary Cisneros held up the churches of Mapleton-Fall Creek as models of urban ministry, members of those churches themselves know well that theirs has generally been a ministry *to* the neighbors more than a ministry *with* the neighbors, despite their efforts to the contrary.

There need be no condescension in such a description. Social critics should think twice before looking down their noses at people who are *only* doing good rather than forming more intimate social bonds. The latter is much more difficult than commonly acknowledged (the white churches of Mapleton-Fall Creek still have very few black members and so, by inference, few members from the neighborhood). But if intimate social bonds, the kind of communication and trust related to social capital, are the goal, then there is reason to believe that a different kind of congregation offers that to inner-city neighborhoods.

One ought not romanticize the connection between smaller congregations and poorer neighborhoods or between black congregations and the black neighborhoods where they are located. In truth, all kinds of congregations have members who drive in from outside the neighborhood. Moreover, class and education segregate members from neighbors both within and among racial or ethnic groups. But it is important to be clear about the difference between social services and economic development on the one hand, and community-building on the other. The better-off congregations do most of the former; and virtually by definition, they do not draw their members from poorer neighborhoods even when their houses of worship are located there. Conversely, some social network connections are uniquely dependent on sharing proximity, race, social class, and worship traditions; but these may not be directly tied to programs for social services or economic development (Farnsley 2000a).

This story of urbanization, involving as it does two stereotypical "inner-city" neighborhoods, provides a dramatic look at how historical circumstance shapes the kind of congregations present in a neighborhood and the role they will play in the development of community or the delivery of social services. Other distinctions can be equally or even more important. The difference between a neighborhood dominated by an established Catholic parish and one filled with a variety of Protestant groups is substantial. Ethnic differences also have a bearing on religious ecology in neighborhood life.

The Mapleton-Fall Creek and Martindale-Brightwood example is especially compelling because it describes two very different religious ecologies operating in apparently similar neighborhoods. But there are important and less dramatic differences in other religious ecologies. The point is not that we must all abandon the notion that congregations are somehow especially connected to the neighborhood around their house of worship. The point is that not every congregation is connected in this way, and more importantly, those that are may have very different kinds of connections.

In the mid-1990s, Mapleton-Fall Creek began a massive redevelopment project that is changing the demographic characteristics of the neighborhood—especially race and income—even as this is written. For many of the reasons described above, this inner-city neighborhood was subject to more rapid change through an infusion of external resources than other urban neighborhoods might have been. The two neighborhoods seem once again to be diverging, making the point even more clearly that demographic descriptions of any "inner-city neighborhood" represent only moments in time, telling us little about where they have come from, where they are headed, or how community organizations—including congregations—fit into that trajectory. We must get behind the demography to understand the organizational ecology of community.

## Are Congregations Local?

Like most good questions, the question of whether or not congregations are really local organizations is multifaceted and complex. To some extent all congregations are local in the sense that they occupy a particular place and cannot help but affect the local environment at least in some small way. However, it is a grievous mistake to assume that congregations are neighborhood-based organizations that exist as assets on which the local neighbors can draw. In an era of asset-based thinking about communities (McKnight and Kretzmann 1993), it is important to insist loudly and often that many congregations are not strong community assets because they are not closely linked to their geographical communities.

Those who continue to describe congregations as local assets and who encourage civic leaders to seek partnership with them in the delivery of services or in community development would do well to consider the several factors noted above. What kind of local connections does the congregation really have? Are the links primarily historical, or is it still actively engaged in local life? Is the mission one of neighbors helping one another, or of members who live elsewhere aiding strangers who live around the house of worship?

Full consideration of these factors requires careful attention to the neighborhood environment in question. What role congregations intend to fill and what role they likely *can* fill is more determined by external circumstance than many proponents of faith-based reforms have been willing to admit.

Of course, the relationship between local circumstances and any particular congregation's mission goals is not simply a matter of happenstance. It is possible for some person or organization in a neighborhood—whether in congregations themselves, in nonprofit service groups, in community groups, or in local government—to attempt to take on the role of gatekeeper. These gatekeepers can serve as conduits for information, building trust and cooperation among the many different urban actors, each relatively unfamiliar with the other's goals and tactics. Such gatekeepers are especially important to organizations that lack the insider knowledge and administrative expertise needed to participate in successful urban partnerships. As Chapter 5 will show, most congregations fall squarely into that camp.

In that world of urban partnership, congregations must be seen as pieces—and often small, edge pieces—of a much larger community puzzle. All of them have some local connection, but few of them are the strong neighborhood actors frequently envisioned in discussions about the role religious organizations might play in urban renewal.

# 5   Is Smaller Better?

Federal policy should reject the failed formula of towering, distant bureaucracies that too often prize process over performance. . . . Traditional social
programs are often too bureaucratic, inflexible, and impersonal to meet the
acute and complex needs of the poor. . . . We will encourage Federal agencies
to become more hospitable to grass-roots and small scale programs, both secular and faith-based, because they have unique strengths that government can't
duplicate. (Bush 2001)

It has become commonplace in America today to bemoan the inefficiencies
of large-scale bureaucracies. Who, after all, wants to be in favor of unnecessary levels of management and continuous entanglements of red tape? There is
genuine disagreement in America concerning the government's role in solving
social problems, but few are now arguing that greater control by federal government, complete with enormous bureaucratic machinery, is the answer to our
most persistent social problems.

Some government programs at the federal level are widely acknowledged to
have achieved goals that local programs could not. For instance, most people,
no matter how conservative, are prepared to concede that the civil rights initiatives associated with the Great Society programs of the 1960s advanced racial
integration more rapidly than local activity could have hoped to do. The point
is not that full racial equality was established, but that the efforts of the federal
government were catalytic.

At the same time, most people, no matter how liberal, are also prepared to
concede that the federal War on Poverty did not work out as well. There can be
no doubt that some goals, most notably a significant decrease in poverty among
the elderly, are linked to Social Security. But some kinds of poverty have proved
resistant to federal intervention. Current welfare reform movements and community development initiatives both reflect a widely held opinion that these activities might be better handled at the level of states, counties, cities, or even
neighborhoods.

One assumption driving this movement toward the smaller, more local level
of administration for programs is the Catholic principle of subsidiarity. Put
most simply, the principle of subsidiarity states that the least complex organization capable of meeting a social need should do so. Or, put another way, social
arrangements should be only as hierarchical and bureaucratic as they *must* be
but no more.

The principle of subsidiarity strikes most of us as just plain common sense.

Just as no one wants to argue that we need large federal programs for their own sake, neither is anyone claiming that big, complex programs are good in and of themselves. The burden is on anyone who wishes to ratchet bureaucracy and administration up a notch, to remove some program or initiative further from the local source, to argue that only at some higher level of management can the issue be adequately addressed.

But even once one grants the validity of the principle and agrees that the burden of proof is on those who argue for less localized, less specific control, the issue is not settled. As in every moral debate, more than principles are at stake. The hard empirical work of determining the level of agency at which social goals can be accomplished must still be done. Reasonable people can agree to subsidiarity in principle and still disagree about the level of organization necessary to the task at hand. Neither smaller nor larger organizations are goods in and of themselves; both are merely tactics for achieving desirable social outcomes.

Recent movement toward welfare reform is a case in point. Widespread social distrust of large federal programs to redistribute income is well documented. One recommended solution has been to push the issue down a level of administration by making block grants to the states and letting the states administer their own programs. The money is still collected and redistributed at the federal level, so the problems associated with social welfare are still considered worthy of national attention. One state can still get back less than it paid in, while another gets more—a redistribution justified by an appeal to fairness in the use of national resources. But responsibility for administering the funds—essentially for deciding what programs work best and who most deserves help—has moved to the state level. There are now considerable differences among states in approaches to welfare service delivery (Carlson-Theis 2000; Demko 1997).

The logic of block grants is that states, because they are smaller and understand their local constituencies better, can deliver the funds and provide services more efficiently than the federal government. The logic assumes that the best way to address poverty differs from Wisconsin to New Jersey to Georgia, an assumption that seems true enough on its face. This same logic works its way down the administrative chain to ever more local, more specific levels of jurisdiction. If states know the needs of their residents better than the federal government, then might not cities and towns know the nuances of their local situation better than states? After all, a metropolitan area with full employment might wish to deliver services or create social incentives that are different than those needed in a town with high unemployment. Economic as well as familial or racial circumstances are truly local in some ways, so there is a convincing argument that local government can better make judgments about local circumstances. If towns and cities can make better decisions than states, perhaps townships or neighborhoods could make even better decisions about local circumstances than could cities or towns. And perhaps very local organizations, such as community centers, community development corporations, and congregations, could make more nuanced, context-specific decisions still. After all, these organizations are presumed to know the specific needs, attached to real faces, experienced by their neighbors.

As argued in Chapter 4, the degree to which congregations, at least, know their local neighbors is frequently overstated, although some are undoubtedly closely tied to local circumstances. But even for those who are local actors with local knowledge, does it then follow from the principle of subsidiarity that they are best able to serve the needs either of local residents or of the entire local community?

At this point, the conversation must move beyond theory about the principle of subsidiarity to a description of actual events. Our society has already acknowledged, at least tacitly, that it is willing to consider the appropriate level of service coordination and delivery without assuming that the smallest unit is always preferable. After all, the logic of subsidiarity by itself presses toward the idea that each individual, or perhaps each family, should simply manage its own resources. If the logic is that more local knowledge of details is better, who knows the most local, specific circumstances better than the families or individuals in need? But it is clear—to most people anyhow—that those individuals in need often cannot sufficiently help themselves without some outside support. If they could, the question of individual or community services would be moot.

So the practical, empirical question becomes, What is the level of organization best able to provide needed support with the most respect for the specificity of each situation and with the most efficient use of scarce resources? The federal government is thought by many to have poor local knowledge and too much administration. Perhaps the same is true for states, or even for cities and towns. The turn toward congregations and other third-sector organizations is offered as a solution to this social dilemma.


## Risks Associated with Congregations as Community Builders or Service Providers

There is no question that congregations, or even denominations, are not administrative bureaucracies on the level of state of federal government. Some religious groups are very hierarchical, but they are still more flexible than public organizations.

But even at the most general level, it is worth asking whether administration and bureaucracy is always bad and organizational flexibility always unambiguously good. If one takes a broad look at Indianapolis, it would be easy to see that two of the most effective community-based organizations are the Catholic Church and the Salvation Army. That does not make Indianapolis an anomaly. These groups are widely acknowledged as effective in cities and towns across the country.

These organizations collect resources, redistribute some of those resources from places that have more to places that have less, and help both individuals and communities in need. But it would be difficult to find two religious organizations that are more bureaucratic and hierarchical in their administration. On the face of it, at least, there is something to be said for organizational structure.

But perhaps the success of the diocese and the Salvation Army is related more to their size than to administration per se. That is, perhaps service effectiveness requires a certain critical mass, and administration and bureaucracy are endemic to size rather than goods in and of themselves.

The issue of size raises critical questions that must be considered under the principle of subsidiarity. It is clearly not the case that smaller is always better, just as it is clear that bigger is not always preferable. When thinking about religious groups, then, evaluation of their community effectiveness must take into account how big the individual units—the congregations—are and how tightly connected they are to the other organizations in their universe (Byrd 1997).

## Actual Practice

There is an abundance of evidence that congregations have difficulty sustaining community development or delivering social welfare services. One of the best examples of the problems encountered in service delivery is the Faith and Families program.

First tried in the state of Mississippi, Faith and Families attempted to match one family needing services with one congregation capable of providing those services. The idea has instinctive appeal. After all, most of us would agree that people who need welfare services do not, as a rule, simply need money. They are in their current state because they lack the ability to care fully for themselves and their family. Of course, few of us are really rugged individualists who do it all for ourselves. We have a variety of support networks—through our family, our neighbors, our congregations, and our schools—that help us through. People who need welfare services lack, by definition, enough support to get by. Matching those people with a congregation is a way of building in that support (Bartkowski et al. 1999).

Faith and Families has been transplanted to Indianapolis with the support of Mayor Goldsmith. Although the program receives only moral support from the city, it is clear that the city built the program in as part of its reform efforts. "The effort is based on the principle that churches can do a significantly better job than government in providing direction and support for families seeking to get off AFDC," said Goldsmith. "We realize that the true grassroots method to reforming welfare is through the community of faith, not government" (Goldsmith 1998).

The goal in Indianapolis, as in Mississippi, is to go beyond the delivery of services to a new level of community support. Said the executive director of the Indianapolis Faith and Families initiative: "A lot of the people don't have acquaintances who own their businesses. Part of what we're doing is introducing families to a networking system."

Faith and Families is the sort of program that makes sense in principle, but its practice has been less than spectacular. In the first two and half years that the program operated in Mississippi, only ninety-eight families volunteered for the program, and these were certainly among the most motivated of welfare recipients. Only twenty-one families were able to remove themselves from the public assistance rolls.

In Indianapolis, the results were similarly modest. Relatively few congregations ever joined the program, and, with the exception of a couple of Catholic parishes and one synagogue, virtually all of these were drawn from middle-class, mainline Protestant traditions. Little outside funding was raised. When Mayor Goldsmith left office, the group lacked the bully pulpit to draw attention to its efforts.

The problem is not only the reluctance of welfare families to participate, at least some of which is due to a reluctance to attend church or get involved in religious activities. A greater problem is congregations' ability to sustain ongoing, effective assistance for the families they adopt. Said one urban community minister in Indianapolis:

> Most churches are set up to help in some way. They see a single mother who needs a job, so they help her find one. But then she cannot get to work without a car, so they help her get a car. But then it turns out that she misses work because of a chemical dependency, which is linked to her mental illness. Her kids are having trouble at school because they are abused and, as it turns out, so was she as a child. Congregations do not have the ability to deal with multiple, reinforcing problems like that.

Moreover, even seemingly small amounts, such as the cost of a car, prove difficult for many congregations to manage. Although people living in poverty do need the sort of moral and networking support that a congregation offers, they also have tangible material needs that congregations cannot usually meet.

Similar problems arise when congregations get involved in the community development business. In the early 1990s, the Lilly Endowment undertook a grant program to sponsor community development efforts in which congregations were included as partners. As is so often true, most of the programs had not become self-sustaining by the end of the grant period and could not function effectively without some other sort of grant assistance.

A professional evaluation of congregations' roles in the effort made the case clearly. Some congregations were interested in these programs and could contribute meaningfully as partners. But the other partners in these housing and economic development ventures often looked to congregations for the wrong things. The other partners wanted help with money and with technical assistance, neither of which congregations often have to spare. What congregations bring instead is moral (and occasionally political) clout, volunteers, and, maybe most importantly, credibility. Partners in this venture, including the congregations themselves, needed to be honest about the reality of what each group brought to the table (Lilly Endowment 1994). In truth, congregations have many fewer financial or volunteer resources than are often attributed to them. The fact that a few congregations have great resources obscures this fact, but the average, ordinary congregation has its hands full just meeting the worship and religious education needs of its members.

Because congregations are being drawn into the social service arena, different groups are attempting to estimate the capacity of congregations to serve. So little is currently known about congregations by the broader public, however, that there is considerable risk that faulty information is finding its way into public discourse.

Indianapolis provides an excellent example of that risk. As cited earlier, a Partners for Sacred Places study of architecturally and historically significant churches in Indianapolis concluded that each of these contributed $144,000 annually to the local community. A closer look at the urban context and congregations' roles in the organizational ecology showed the problems associated with such generalizations. A different survey by the Urban Institute of metropolitan Washington, D.C., congregations found that the average faith community there spent $14,000 on social services. That number is entirely plausible as an *average*, taking the sample as a whole; and it is, of course, roughly 10 percent of the $144,000 figure from Indianapolis (Boris and Printz 1997; Printz 1998).

But even $14,000 is probably high. The average congregation in the Urban Institute sample had 400 members. Our work in Indianapolis, and other national studies as well, put median congregational size at closer to 100 to 150. So the Washington sample may have been skewed toward larger groups, as would not be surprising in a survey.

Still, $14,000 is a ballpark figure. Indeed, our figures in Indianapolis put the average social service spending by congregations at closer to $19,000 for the 60 percent of congregations that have provided amounts for us (acknowledging that larger congregations who spend the most money are most likely to report their budgets). Since we have good reasons to believe that the 40 percent that did not provide figures spend considerably less than the average, we believe the true average to be lower.

Debate over a few thousand dollars takes us far from the point here. In truth, a typical congregation spends far less than this average. Indeed, the average is propped up by a relatively small number of congregations with many well-funded social services programs. And in those cases, some of the funding is already coming from grants or from government contracts and not from the beneficence of members themselves.

In our total sample, the top 20 percent of social service spenders provided 80 percent of the funds. In the inner city, the top 10 percent spent 90 percent of the money. A typical congregation spends something more like $1,000–$3,000 on social services. A typical congregation, therefore, is going to find a complex, involved relationship with even one needy family difficult to manage.

At this point, the principle of subsidiarity comes into much clearer focus. The advantages of social support networks to needy families or individuals are clear enough. But congregations often lack the resources to deal effectively with even one needy family. Unfortunately, nearly 7,000 Indianapolis families received Temporary Assistance to Needy Families (TANF) in the most recent count, with more than 55,000 per month receiving food stamps. So if the principle of subsidiarity demands that we search for the least bureaucratic, most locally oriented level of organization capable of addressing an issue, honesty compels us to admit that congregations could never be more than a small part of the solution.

## Administrative Necessity

Congregations seeking a larger role in the community development and social service arena face some hard realities almost immediately. In each of the Indianapolis-based initiatives intended to draw greater congregational involvement and support, congregations were required to write grants, define administrative plans for programs, and think critically about evaluation of their efforts. Sometimes congregations were competing with other organizations for available money or other program assistance. Many congregations have had difficulty writing effective grants or planning manageable programs.

The first, and in some ways most straightforward, example of congregations entering a strange new world was the effort by Marion County Juvenile Court Judge James Payne to enlist congregations as case workers for juveniles sentenced to home-based counseling. Payne was explicitly following the logic set forth by Marvin Olasky in his book *The Tragedy of American Compassion* (1992). Olasky argues that the movement of charity or services out of the private sector, especially the religious sector, and into state-controlled bureaucratic programs has been a social disaster. Efficiency—measured by funds spent and number of clients served—became the bureaucratic goals rather than effective change of troubled lives, one life at a time.

Judge Payne put the word out that he would be accepting applications from congregations. In lingo familiar to any social service professional, his office announced that they were issuing a Request for Proposals, commonly known as RFPs. After a couple of months, the judge's office sponsored an informational meeting to discuss how the grant proposals were to look. They emphasized to the congregations that bureaucratic neatness and proper formatting were not all that important. What they really needed to know was how the congregation would serve the juvenile and the family and how they would meet a few simple reporting criteria that measured number of visits, number of hours spent with the child, and so on. After a careful, straightforward presentation of the plan, the judge opened the floor to questions. The first question was telling: "What's an RFP?"

When the proposals finally came in, they demonstrated that the question was not asked facetiously. Many of the congregations were unable to write program guidelines that met even the most streamlined, simplified criteria required by law. Many did not specify how the child would be counseled. Others did not make clear how many visits would be made or how many times per week the visits would come.

Most importantly, however, most congregations were unable to write grants that matched the scope of activities suggested. One might expect that congregations wrote grants that fell far short of the court's expectations, but in fact the opposite was true. Judge Payne had imagined that congregations would write grants showing how they would deal with one child assigned to their care. The assumption was that they, rather than a professional social worker, would take responsibility for this child. At the end of the contract, they would get paid the $2,400 that would otherwise have gone to an individual professional or to an agency. If all went well, they would get assigned another child. After a pattern of successes, they might be assigned multiple children.

What the court got instead were many applications that explained how a congregation, or some sort of coalition, would deal with twenty or fifty or one hundred children. The applications were loaded with overhead—everything from hiring a program director and a secretary; to finding new office space; to buying the needed technology such as copiers, fax machines, and cellular phones.

What the court found was that many congregations were willing to take responsibility for such an effort only if they could develop the professional apparatus with which to do it. Most could not imagine their congregation taking this on as a simple, one-time adoption of a particular child. They were thinking of programs and new professionals to help them do this. Even when congregations suggested that they would provide volunteer families to mentor the juveniles, they still wanted to hire program directors to manage the operations.

The judge's office was not the only place that experienced initial disappointment as it tried to bring congregations in as partners in civic activities. The Coalition for Homelessness Intervention and Prevention (CHIP) received a substantial grant from the Lilly Endowment, $2.7 million dollars, to fund demonstration projects around several issues related to homelessness in the city. $500,000 of that was earmarked for programs that involved congregations as partners in efforts to build and maintain transitional housing.

Unlike Judge Payne's office, which relied on an existing administrator to work with the congregations, CHIP hired two professional social workers to oversee the writing of planning grants, the writing of full proposals by those selected for planning grants, and the implementation of projects by the eventual grantees. In effect, someone was appointed—with a salary set aside for this purpose—to act as a gatekeeper for this small subset of congregations.

The story of CHIP shows just how small the universe of congregations prepared to move into the social service and development arena really is. CHIP was not doling out small grants of a few thousand dollars. They were making substantial $150,000 grants to fund large demonstration projects. In the end, their initial RFP did not attract enough good applications for them to fund. They funded only two groups at the outset, although they worked with a third organization until its application was strong enough to be approved.

The groups that received funding tell the story. One is the largest congregation in Indianapolis—a 10,000-member African-American Missionary Baptist Church. This group was prepared to spend what it took to implement its transitional housing program and had assigned a staff member to this task to act as its own gatekeeper. Only a handful of congregations in the city would have been capable of such a move.

The second group funded at the outset was a coalition of middle-class churches in a neighborhood that was gradually shifting, at the edges, toward poorer neighbors. This coalition, though still in its organizational infancy, was reasonably well connected to CHIP and to eastside community groups. They were able to hire a consultant to help them write their grant proposal, and this person eventually became a CHIP employee with responsibility for overseeing the Congregations as Partners Project.

The third congregation eventually to be funded was another very large congregation already engaged in a number of development projects in an African-American neighborhood. They were involved in every grant competition available at the time, designating potential funding from each source as "leveraged funds" they could promise the other sources. They had the support of the mayor's office and were, in fact, the venue he had chosen when Rev. Eugene Rivers came from Boston to speak to the Indianapolis community.

To date, sponsors of these congregational partnerships seem relatively pleased with early progress. But most of the faith-based partnerships proved more difficult to get off the ground than the secular providers had imagined. The Front Porch Alliance foundered when the new Democratic mayor did not support it. But even when the experiments do meet with modest success, it is important to recognize how few congregations are involved. Moreover, it is crucial to recognize how little of their own money or organizational expertise congregations bring to the table in the new partnerships.

The point is not to criticize people who are trying to do good by implying that it is still not enough. But these early efforts get to the heart of the subsidiarity issue. The principle of subsidiarity suggests that the small size of congregations is an advantage for them because they can be more flexible and less bureaucratically constrained as they deal with local problems. The reality of the situation is that most congregations are much too small to have a broad impact and are too small, even, to write the grant applications or leverage the funds necessary to compete in the public or foundation funding arena.

It is clear, therefore, that if most congregations are to provide services that require money, then the way money is made available to them will have to change. In Indianapolis, they are looking to the Lilly Endowment and to public money that usually passes through the city. Or perhaps it is better to say that, in some cases at least, the Endowment, the city, and even the juvenile court is looking to them.

If congregations must enter the contest for these external dollars, then they are faced with the daunting prospect of writing grants, administering programs, and evaluating their efforts. In that sphere, the fact that congregations lack bureaucracy and administration is much less of a virtue. Professional service organizations receive grants precisely because they have the administration necessary to write grants and operate programs as well as the expertise to evaluate their efforts.

Grant proposals from congregations to date make it clear that they understand this dilemma, at least tacitly. More than a few have written grants for funds with which to hire grant writers to compete for future, ostensibly larger, funding. RFPs designed to draw them in as one-on-one caseworkers have been met with proposals to develop new professional organizations capable of doing the necessary administration, even if the administration is of volunteer help.

Most congregations do not have the money to support more than the ad hoc efforts they already undertake. If they are to enter the world of public or civic funding, either they will develop the administrative capacity to do this or—and this is considerably less likely—the funders will soften or even suspend their requirements about grant writing, administration, or evaluation.

The latter concept is not entirely far-fetched. At least a couple of small, street-based programs in Indianapolis received both financial and moral support from the Goldsmith administration. Mayor Goldsmith's claim was clear: these neighborhood activists and entrepreneurs are best-suited to the task before them because of who they are and what they do; the fact that they are not good grant writers or administrators should not count against them.

While such a concept works in principle, it is difficult to imagine either the government or even private foundations making substantial grants without administrative requirements. Doubtless there is room for some give-and-take on this issue, and some middle ground may still be reached. But congregations and funders are, at present, still far apart on issues of administrative efficiency and competence. The degree to which they move closer together is the degree to which congregations lose some of the supposed advantages of subsidiarity. Moreover, without the support of the mayor's bully pulpit, will there be enough incentive to take the necessary risks?

## Local Ecology Again

At this point, it becomes even clearer that all of the potential partners need good information about the other organizations in their community's social ecology. On the one hand, potential partners in government or foundations must understand the dynamics of the congregations with which they would work. It is futile to expect small, independent congregations to muster the same administrative resources as ones that are large and well-funded or tied to substantial bureaucracies with access to management expertise. Similarly, it is futile to imagine that public/private partnerships will work the same in a city dominated by, say, a strong Catholic diocese and a majority Catholic population, as it will in a city dominated by relatively unconnected Protestant congregations. Moreover, there is likely to be understandable resistance to any specific programs when religious diversity—especially non-Christian diversity—is greater.

Congregations, for their part, stand little chance if they do not have some basic conception of how local government and existing local service organizations operate. Groups that do not have full-time community ministers—and fewer than 1 percent have such a person—are unlikely to have much knowledge of the other congregations or the secular service organizations in their community. It is possible, after all, to be too small and too concerned about internal congregational affairs to be able to keep up either with the paperwork or with the breadth of local activities.

Again, the concept of information gatekeepers who have the support of city government, local foundations, and the local business community makes sense here. If public-private partnerships are to work, and especially if they are to work with relatively small religious organizations such as congregations, then some person or organization must serve as the conduit for information and expertise. Otherwise, the proposed assets of congregations—even their flexibility as unbounded organizations—will likely prove to be liabilities. Organizations like CHIP, with a large grant from the Lilly Endowment via United Way, or congregations like the large Missionary Baptist Church with substantial internal funding, may be able to supply their own gatekeepers to serve this conduit function with a specific interest in mind. But who will pay for the civil servants capable of bridging the government, the social service community, and the congregations with the interest of particular neighborhoods in mind?

## Is It All About Money?

Some will be inclined to argue that the emphasis on money—whether in grant writing or evaluation—is misplaced. What congregations offer is different, they might argue, and ultimately it is even more important than money. Congregations provide moral support, political clout, presumed legitimacy, and a steady stream of volunteers to efforts with which they are involved.

Volunteer help is the easiest to measure of the "intangibles" that congregations offer. There can be no doubt that congregations provide volunteers for a variety of efforts in the community. However, it is important to temper enthusiasm for that volunteer effort with a healthy dose of reality about congregational members. Overall, 29 percent of the members are over 55 years of age. In the inner city and near suburbs (usually founded immediately after World War II), the average age is slightly higher. Overall, about 60 percent of congregational members are women. In some inner-city neighborhoods, that number is closer to 70 percent.

Therefore, much of the volunteer help coming from congregations is coming from elderly women. Although no one would argue that these volunteers do not make positive contributions, they do not fit very well with the sort of projects that have been calling most forcefully for congregational help. Elderly women are not best suited to working with juvenile delinquents (the majority of whom are boys), providing summer programs for youth, or building transitional housing for the homeless.

Here again, the relatively small size and unrepresentative populations in many congregations may be more of a hindrance than a help. These groups may not bureaucratically constrained, but they are constrained both by available resources and by the nature of who they are and what they can reasonably accomplish.

Congregations can provide moral support and a kind of presumptive legitimacy to efforts going on in a neighborhood and can thereby be effective partners, but the degree to which they can do this is tied to their "local" affiliation as discussed in Chapter 3. Not all congregations have a deep well of local moral capital. Some are not even regarded as assets in their neighborhoods.

## Congregations as Partners

Given the limitations congregations face, limitations that often outweigh the advantages of being flexible and relatively small, it makes sense to consider the ways in which congregations could function as partners with other organizations. Under the right circumstances, congregations do bring certain advantages, including a presumed moral legitimacy, to activities they support. How can the strengths of congregations be best matched with other organizational strengths that help address congregational weaknesses?

One working model involves neighborhood partnerships formed around virtual "territorial parishes" (Bos 1993). In this model, several congregations work together to serve a defined area. They may each operate different small programs to which they mutually refer, or they may pool resources to offer some joint programming either at one of their sites or at some neutral location.

Several elements seem crucial to the success of neighborhood-based partnerships involving congregations. There tend to be at least three, and usually more, congregations who have agreed on a common territory or service area, usually a neighborhood. Although the partnerships seem to involve three or more congregations, it is not unusual for one, or perhaps two of those groups to bring most of the resources to the table in the beginning. Most territorial parishes have made significant efforts to involve as many congregations as will join, even if these others have limited resources.

In many cases, there is a cooperative effort among the congregations and some local, noncongregational services group. In many neighborhoods the local church coalition works with a community center, a neighborhood association, a community development corporation, or some combination thereof to coordinate services and programs. This partnership among congregations and other community groups is especially important for the free flow of good, practical information. Professionals in community groups like community development corporations (CDCs) or community centers usually have much better information from the city or from the nonprofit community and are often well-suited to work as gatekeepers, especially if they have a foothold in the local faith community. They usually work with other sorts of community data, such as demographics or social service statistics, that are foreign to pastors and to many laypeople. From the local side, neighborhood associations provide information about specific concerns such as trash collection, policing, street use, or disputes among renters and owners. All of that information can go unrecognized by a congregation unless a high concentration of its members live in the surrounding area.

Connections among congregations and other community groups also help build access to resources, especially to money. Community development and social service professionals know more about grant writing and, at least as importantly, about where the available money is to begin with. The more congregations tap this source, the more they add the resource they most often lack.

The obverse of this is that congregations sometimes provide local community organizations with interpersonal networks that reach far beyond the neighborhood. Although we have argued that congregations do not draw as many of their members from the local neighborhood as is frequently assumed, that is not unambiguously a disadvantage. Although it is true that a large drive-in membership makes it more difficult for a congregation to build community connections locally or to benefit from nuanced local knowledge, the corresponding benefit is that some of the drive-in members "drive in" from places with greater resources and offer connections to those resources. To put it another way, it is not always bad that congregations in a poor neighborhood have members who come from places with more money and more social power. Sometimes a neighborhood's connections at the city offices, at the foundation headquarters, or with businesses are built through the personal networks and connections of individuals whose only connection to this neighborhood is through their church attendance there.

A variation on this theme can be seen in the sort of suburban-urban linkages that have been cropping up in Indianapolis. Although some denominations, notably the United Methodists and the Catholic archdiocese, move funds from the "haves" to the "have-nots" through their organizational apparatus, other congregations have developed direct place-to-place connections.

Most of these connections have been a single suburban congregation offering support to a single urban congregation involved in what is typically called "urban ministry." And more often than not, this connection is usually about money or, at most, about money and occasional volunteer help. One large Presbyterian church in Indianapolis has, in years past, sent as much as $100,000 per year to support the social programs of an inner-city Presbyterian congregation that raises something closer to $40,000 per year in its own tithes and offerings.

But sometimes the connections go beyond this basic mission work. In at least a few cases, suburban churches have actually donated members, sometimes for specified amounts of time, to inner-city churches. That is, the members will shift membership for a period of one or two years. In this way, the networks and other interpersonal resources of a suburban congregation become available, at least indirectly, to their urban counterpart. More to the point, the process becomes a learning experience for both parties, thus breaking the stereotype of noblesse oblige in which all of the advantages and strengths are thought to run in one direction.

In another case, the suburban congregation was originally a mission outpost of the large, urban congregation that was now part of the inner city. The relationship was seen as truly reciprocal, with both groups addressing needs as they saw them in the social environment of the time, despite the fact that the environment had changed significantly.

In yet another case, a suburban congregation developed a partnership, not with a specific urban congregation, but with a territorial coalition as described above. This partnership, the Community Resurrection Partnership of Martindale-Brightwood, now includes a community development corporation, a community center, a local bank, a very large suburban congregation with multiple resources, and several local congregations in the neighborhood itself. It is impossible to say what will come of the Community Resurrection Partnership, but it at least seems designed to benefit from the strengths of each of its partners without expecting them to display strengths that they are unlikely to have.

Mayor Goldsmith's office, under the auspices of the Front Porch Alliance (FPA), played an interesting role in the formation of these new partnerships. When the mayor first began thinking about working with congregations, he planned to do what, from a politician's standpoint, made the most sense. He intended to announce a policy initiative in a neighborhood and then to encourage all the local congregations to get on the bandwagon.

Such a plan was never put into place, however, because neighborhoods that were not included balked, and because other noncongregational community organizations insisted on being included. Instead, the FPA became a clearinghouse for neighborhood groups, especially congregations, that were trying to start programs aimed at human service delivery or some sort of economic or community development. The FPA became the office a pastor called if he was thinking about starting a summer recreation program or if he wanted a crack house across the street from his church closed down. Congregations that wanted to start programs or to get involved with existing programs used this arm of the mayor's office to find out what was what.

Because the FPA had the resources of city hall at its disposal, it was able to help congregations in ways that other organizations could not. No other group could bring the benefits of police activity, especially under the auspices of local "community policing" programs, to a congregation so quickly. No other group could arrange for changes in zoning or curfew or trash pick-up so directly.

Most importantly, however, the FPA was able to put congregations, especially small black congregations in inner-city neighborhoods, in touch with money and other program resources that they most needed. When Judge Payne's office put out their Request for Proposals, members of the FPA offered support and encouragement to congregations who were thinking of applying. The director of FPA essentially wrote one congregation's grant proposal and consulted on others.

When CHIP put out their Request for Proposals, the FPA was there again. Its director not only served as a proposal referee, but he also actively endorsed the efforts of several congregations working with the FPA. In at least one instance, the grant proposal involved concessions from the city in some public housing properties. Coordination of interests through the FPA made the deal work. But the most direct linkage between congregations and the city involved the funds, both federal and local, that passed through city government to service providers. For example, the mayor's office sponsored a "Porchlight" grant program for neighborhood groups hoping to sponsor summer activities for children. A number of congregations received money from the city in that endeavor.

More telling, however, was the number of congregations that came to the table for the first time seeking pass-through federal funds. Each year, Indianapolis receives block grants from the Department of Housing and Urban Development (HUD), some of which are earmarked for very specific social activities. The largest pool in this group is known as Community Development Block Grants (CDBGs). In 1998, with the support of FPA, several congregations applied for the first time for federal funding to support their social programs or housing development.

The linkage between city support via the FPA and congregations cannot be overstated. In every instance—juvenile court, CHIP, HUD grants—the FPA lent its credibility to small programs that had not written effective grants and that had little hope of administering or evaluating programs in the manner to which both the federal government and the Lilly Endowment were accustomed. The FPA made the argument that the most effective workers in distressed neighborhoods were not necessarily those who played the game of grant writing and program evaluation, but those who knew the streets. They argued, perhaps a little romantically, that these people were getting results even if those results were hard to document.

This line of argument, and this linkage between the city and the programs of small congregations with few ties to social power in Indianapolis, deserves much more attention than it has received to date. The most significant problem facing small congregations interested in community work is that they have more ideas than money. No matter how successful they are, it is difficult to get the money unless one can document that success in the interest of writing better applications. Put another way, one has to get that initial credibility somewhere.

Government and foundations are not being obtuse when they insist on these standards. It would be very easy to bluff about one's success in working with inner city kids or drug addicts or homeless mothers, populations about which often too little is known, especially by potential funders. More than one government agency or private funder has given money to a "poverty pimp" who trumpets concern for clients but spends the money unwisely and has few measurable —other than rhetorical—results.

The FPA circumvented such problems, at least to some extent, by lending its credibility to the efforts of inner-city congregations. It made the de facto claim that these programs were working and that lives were being changed. It told funders, including itself, what everyone wanted to hear: these "neighborhood Josephs," as Robert Woodson (1998) has called them, are the answer. We need, said the city, to support and encourage their efforts with the least red tape and bureaucracy.

But the spark and the legitimacy of the Front Porch Alliance came from Mayor Goldsmith's philosophical commitment to it. He genuinely wished to strengthen the nongovernmental sector's ability to provide the institutional bases for community life. As his administration dissolved, however, it became clear that the same moral and financial support would not be forthcoming from the new mayor. There is good reason to believe that many of these fledgling initiatives will die without constant tending by the city. Even though the city's ultimate goal was to make its support less necessary, that process would take years, if not generations, and its growth now seems stunted.

## The Changing Social Climate

All of the efforts discussed above are linked together as part of a national shift in the way we think about congregations as social actors. The most notable change at the federal level has been the Charitable Choice provision attached to certain kinds of federal funding. What Charitable Choice says, in essence, is that congregations or other faith-based groups cannot be discriminated against because they practice their faith in the delivery of services (or whatever else they do). Therefore, if any private organization can apply for state funds or can redeem service vouchers distributed by the state, so can congregations. And they can do so *without having to remove religious symbols or to avoid religious language.*

Put that simply, Charitable Choice would seem to be both a bonanza for congregations interested in social ministry and a cesspool for civil rights abuses. The law, however, has tried to deal with the latter. No service client can ever be required to receive services from a faith-based provider of any kind. Essentially, the state must guarantee its clients a secular option. Indeed, a state can choose to deliver all services itself and refuse to contract with any outside providers whatever.

Charitable Choice states only that if private service providers, usually called "vendors" in the business, can bid for contracts or cash vouchers, then so can faith-based groups. And the faith-based groups can practice their faith while delivering services—including religiously based hiring discrimination—so long as their clients choose to be there.

The other limit to Charitable Choice is more technical but ultimately much more important. Charitable Choice originally applied only to the particular block grant program known as TANF, Temporary Assistance to Needy Families. As noted above, a few other programs were gradually included. So the many efforts discussed above do not really fall under this legal provision. But the passage of Charitable Choice and its ongoing discussion in legal and political circles has contributed to the environment in which these other changes are taking place.

Another change at the federal level lends credibility to these local changes. HUD now aggressively pursues faith-based groups, especially congregations, as community and economic development partners. HUD has begun a national initiative aimed at building new faith-based linkages and strengthening existing ones. Under Henry Cisneros, San Antonio's super-mayor counterpart to Steve Goldsmith, HUD started moving toward congregations as the preferable private option in dispossessed communities. It is precisely because faith-based groups have come to the fore in these arenas that it is so important to consider the sociological facts alongside the rhetoric shaping social reform. The rhetoric sometimes pictures congregations as the most locally based groups with the best information about the neighborhood. But as we have seen, what it means to be local is not always clear, and even when definitions are provided, many congregations could not be said to be truly "local."

The rhetoric also emphasizes the virtue of subsidiarity. But as we have seen in this chapter, small size is not always a virtue, especially in a complex environment of program development, fundraising, and administration. Partnerships can work, but they require sober consideration of the contributions congregations will make. Support by a more powerful third party, such as the city, can aid the process, but it also creates alliances and overlap that may have serious consequences, as discussed in Chapter 6.

Perhaps the most sobering reality that must be continually presented is just how few congregations are interested in this sort of work. Judge Payne's Request for Proposals eventually drew twelve proposals, many of which were very poorly written and presented risky chances for success. The concerns were not for the quality of the writing as such but for the lack of administrative competence displayed in the effort.

The Porchlight grant program of the city drew about a hundred applications, but these were for very small amounts—generally less than $5,000—and many were from agencies other than congregations that had supported summer programs for some time and simply found this a source of additional funding. The CHIP initiative drew seven applications, only six of which were seriously considered by the committee at all (five of the six received planning grants). Only one of the CHIP grants involved significant partnerships among several congregations.

Given the scope of poverty and the need for community development in Indianapolis, and also given the fact that there are roughly 1,200 congregations in the city, this is an "underwhelming" response. A few congregations, thought of as individual organizations, will be able to make significant contributions to their neighborhoods and to the wider Indianapolis communities. But congregations as an institutional sphere of activity likely will not. There are neither enough resources nor enough interest from most groups to throw themselves into this complicated social arena.

When policy leaders and urban planner think about the benefits of congregations based on subsidiarity, they must be very careful to note what really exists. Congregations are small relative to government programs, unencumbered by legal restrictions, and flexible in their decision making. But most of them lack not only the administrative ability or the money to tackle a task of this magnitude, but they also lack the inclination. Subsidiarity demands that we look for the smallest institutional and organizational unit capable of achieving a social goal. Reality demands that we acknowledge the severe limitations of congregations' capabilities and view them in the context of the entire organizational field.

# 6    Can Congregations Impart Values?

> Without diminishing the important work of government agencies and the
> wide range of nonprofit service providers, this initiative will support the
> unique capacity of local faith-based and other community programs to serve
> people in need, not just by providing services but also by transforming lives.
> (Bush 2001)

> There is little disagreement that the problems of inner city neighborhoods
> go far beyond simple lack of material wealth. The youth of these areas need
> values and moral structures to hang onto. They need reasons to believe these
> things are worth living for. They need nurturing. Few institutions other than
> the faith community and the family can provide youth this kind of support.
> (Cisneros 1996)

At first, the title of this chapter appears absurd. Of course congregations can
impart values. They have been doing so for centuries. But the question is not
whether a congregation can teach values to its members and to their children,
or even whether a small local parish can influence the villagers for whose spiritual lives it is responsible. At issue here is whether congregations can, in the
course of offering social services or promoting community development, provide spiritual and moral guidance in ways that other service organizations cannot. That is the hope, and often the claim, of those who argue for a broader
congregational role in community life. Such a hope might be taken on faith, but
the claim must be considered empirically.

A pervasive theme in faith-based welfare reform or community development
is the linkage between material poverty and moral or spiritual poverty. Cisneros
said plainly that inner-city problems went far beyond the lack of material wealth
to values and moral structure. Newly elected President George W. Bush was
more cautious just five years later, recognizing that a conservative push to engage the faith community would meet with greater resistance: "Faith-based
groups' programs attack dependency on drugs with faith and love, often helping
men and women for whom conventional treatment seemed to provide little last-
ing help" (2001).

To some impoverished people, this linkage of poverty and dependency with
value-deficiency is an insult. Those of us with economic security must be careful not to link our own morality too closely with our wealth as we judge the
linkage between morality and poverty in others. Nonetheless, there are undeniable connections between the traditional vices—substance abuse, gambling,
physical abuse—and material poverty. Moreover, there is clear enough evidence

that other kinds of behavior, such as single parenthood, have social consequences. One need not make a strenuous judgment about the personal morality
of the individuals involved to see a relationship between single parenting and
poverty. A child growing up with only one parent in America is many times
more likely to live in poverty than is a child with both parents at home.

Practicing some behaviors and avoiding others clearly makes for more productive, more self-sufficient citizens. Equally clearly, congregations are known
to promote good behavior and sanction bad. Therefore, so the argument goes,
congregations could do a better job than other kinds of organizations in providing services in ways that promote and instill the needed values.

However, this logic contains a leap that is too seldom questioned. Congregations are known for promoting good behavior and sanctioning bad among their
own. They are supportive communities that provide moral teaching as well as
both remonstrance and forgiveness. But congregations do this for their *members,* for the people who freely choose to attend or who have personal or familial
ties to the group. The logical leap being made by contemporary reformers is that
congregations can impart values and sanction behavior for those who are not
members. There is little evidence to support or refute this claim because not
nearly enough is known about why some social programs succeed and others
fail. But it is still possible to raise important questions based on what has hap-
pened thus far.

### What Makes Faith-Based Better?

In Indianapolis, both Judge Payne and Mayor Goldsmith made it clear
that they thought faith-based services would be preferable because they would
contain moral content. It was not enough, they contended, to provide material
support. What needy individuals and needy neighborhoods needed most were
strong values and core beliefs wrapped inside the support and nurture of a caring community of faith.

It is easy enough to see the commonsense linkage between religious communities and strong moral values. Most people are prepared to believe that regular
worship attendance is correlated to volunteering, to avoiding juvenile delin-
quency, to charitable giving, and to a host of other socially beneficial activities.
The linkage in and of itself strikes most of us as obvious and needs no further
defense.

But common sense might take us a step farther to ask, What real advantage
will faith-based providers offer the recipients of their services? Having observed
the development of faith-based partnerships in Indianapolis, I noted four central assumptions about the faith-based advantage related to personal values.

First, virtually all proponents of faith-based reforms hope and assume that
congregations and other local, faith-based providers will be able to instill the
social values such as hard work, sobriety, and self-sufficiency. They hope that
religious organizations might succeed where, in their view, secular service or
development efforts have failed (Wallis 1997; DiIulio 1997a).

Second, some proponents of faith-based reforms hope that closer contact with the needy will be a subtle form of evangelism, that by contact with churches, needy individuals and communities might hear and accept the Gospel message. This view is seldom articulated clearly for fear that government or foundation funders will shy away from any association with direct evangelization, but the hope is undeniably present for many who champion these reforms (Olasky 1992; Sherman 1995, 2000).

Third, most proponents of faith-based reform hope that congregations, especially, can serve as surrogate communities and perhaps eventually as real communities for those they serve. Those of us in the middle or upper classes have built-in support systems. If our car breaks down or our daycare provider is ill, or even if we are temporarily unemployed, we have networks of friends and family who have the resources to help us. Poor people and impoverished communities, virtually by definition, have a shortage of support (Olasky 1992; Goldsmith 1998).

Fourth, many proponents of faith-based reforms hope that men from the faith communities, especially pastors, can be strong role models for adolescent males. This hope is strongest in the African-American community, where the percentage of noncustodial fathers is highest, but the clear linkage between one-parent households and poverty cuts across races. There is a deep hope, even an expectation, that congregations can provide a strong father figure in a way that secular social workers cannot.

## Moral Content

We can consider each of these expectations in turn. The clearest expectation and hope, held by virtually any proponent of faith-based reforms of any kind, is that congregations and other religious providers of services or development will add moral content to the lives of the people they encounter. Proponents of faith-based reforms are willing to move resources toward congregation because they believe congregations provide some "value added" to the social work or development equation. When it comes to faith-based groups, the "value added" is values.

What has become clear is that many people see secular welfare provision, linked as it is to government, as content neutral. Most traditional social workers would deny this, claiming that they too promote the general social values of hard work, thrift, good parenting, and so on. But it is clear enough that most Americans see a link between behavior and poverty, even if they admit that some people are poor through no fault of their own. Reasonable people disagree about whether moral behavior is the cause or the effect, but few would deny that poor communities and poor individuals would be better off without drug traffic, without the multitudes of liquor stores, without unwanted pregnancies, and with ideals such as sobriety and self-sufficiency.

Members of religious congregations tend to exhibit these positive qualities and to avoid many of the dysfunctional behaviors. The point is not, of course, that members of congregations are morally perfect or that they shun every vice. The point is that they belong to a community that sets and enforces social standards. The degree of strictness varies from faith community to faith community, but all have moral standards and all provide support, whether by carrot or by stick, for members striving to maintain them.

But it is crucial to remember that those standards are not general or merely social; they are linked to clear religious principles with theological content. Proponents of faith-based social reforms, especially those who argue that congregations should play a larger role, have not been forthcoming enough about the linkage between beneficial character traits and the specific beliefs within any theological worldview. Most Americans care only about the social moral values and see them as common to all faiths. Indeed, there is often a general sense that we do not much care what specific beliefs surround these traits so long as this upright character—hard work, sobriety, parental responsibility—is produced.

But faith-based groups do not teach "values" on Wednesdays and "beliefs" on Saturdays and Sundays. Values are part of the whole package and are, in many faiths, the result of conversion. Once a person's life is right with God, then she begins to exhibit the fruits of the Spirit that make for a good neighbor. Many evangelicals, for instance, would go so far as to say that the many habits of good citizenship do not ultimately matter if the person is still bound for hell.

Roughly a decade ago, an Indianapolis pastor conducted a survey of clergy in the central city area. One of his questions asked what the Bible commanded believers most clearly to do. Some emphasized that they were called to feed the hungry and clothe the naked. Others emphasized that they were to lead people to faith, saying that material needs would be met once the relationship to God was right. But most of the respondents said that they were called to minister to the spiritual, material, and emotional needs of humanity. God's answer was part of a larger package in which these were all interwoven. They wanted to help the poor and dispossessed get their lives on the right track, but the first step in that direction, almost by definition, involved developing a right relationship with God.

Here the waters of faith-based reform get very murky. Not all faith communities make the hard separation between sacred and secular, or between church and state, that social liberals and liberal Christians tend to make. For most of the African-American pastors and their churches involved in faith-based reform in Indianapolis, social services are about content, and the content is Christian. Since an overwhelming majority of African Americans in the city identify themselves as Christian, the issue is not hotly contested within the black community. It has a certain taken-for-granted quality. Moreover, African Americans do not, as a rule, make the same rigid distinction between their religious lives and the rest of their responsibilities in the community.

The kind of survey results presented in Chapter 3 make a compelling case. African-American respondents were 40 percent more likely than white respondents to describe themselves as "very religious or spiritual." They were more than *twice* as likely—63 percent to 30 percent—to say that the Bible was to be

taken literally as the Word of God. On every question about economic or political decisions, from general influence on public policy to specific influence on
the minimum wage, between 75 percent and 85 percent of African Americans
said that religion should be involved, compared to 45 percent to 55 percent for
whites.

The pattern is clear. African Americans are more personally religious than
whites, they see religion as more intertwined with secular life, and they are more
favorably disposed toward placing public funds in the hands of churches. Thus,
the values that African-American congregations would be adding to the development or social services mix are explicitly Christian. That is to say, there is no
sense in which these values are somehow "liberal" or "content neutral," and no
corresponding expectation that they will somehow promote values in general,
if indeed there is any such thing as "values in general."

In other communities, however, the relationship between public and private,
and between religious and secular, has not been so neatly drawn. There is a
vague hope that faith-based groups will build moral character, but there are few
straightforward admissions that this character stems directly from explicitly
Christian evangelization. Thus liberals and Christian conservatives cooperate
uneasily and are seldom closely allied in any specific programs.

The content-specific nature of religious values was not lost on Christian
conservatives. Many responded swiftly and negatively to President George W.
Bush's call for greater public support for faith-based groups because they immediately saw the problems associated, in their minds, with public funding for
religious groups they considered unworthy. There would be no way for the government to discriminate against, say, Muslim providers in relation to Christian
ones. Yet the Rev. Jerry Falwell was clear in his opinion:

> I think the Moslem faith teaches hate. . . . I think that when persons are clearly
> bigoted toward other persons in the human family, they should be disqualified
> from [Charitable Choice] funds. For that reason, Islam should be out the door
> before they knock. (Beliefnet.com 2001)

To be fair, to date these issues have not come up in Indianapolis, a city that
is emphatically not embroiled in multicultural or ethnic tensions. This points
up one more interesting way in which the local ecology—the mix of cultures,
institutions, and even religious traditions—is an important variable to be considered in assessing the potential for public/private partnerships involving the
faith community. In a city with a broad Protestant culture like Indianapolis has,
it is possible, though still not without risks, to proceed in a straightforward fashion, assuming that certain general understandings may be widely held in common. In a more diverse religious environment, ignoring the multicultural stick-
ing points can only lead to distrust and misunderstanding.

At a citywide conference, the pastor of one of the largest community churches
said that he hoped Indianapolis could be a test case for the rest of the nation.
"There is a lot of talk about problems with diversity and complaints about
specific beliefs being pushed," he offered, "but these experiments have been

underway in Indianapolis for some time and we have not seen those problems." While the pastor was right insofar as the Indianapolis experience has been relatively free of controversy, his comments did not account for the overwhelmingly Christian culture of the city. In the grant programs to date, no non-Christian programs had applied for any of the money. His comments also discounted the fact that so far fairly little public money had changed hands or secular social workers displaced, so the stakes were still quite low.

But even in a relatively stable, harmonious situation like Indianapolis's, differences between liberals and evangelicals threaten the alliance between different funding groups and their proposed congregational partners, as we shall see in the next section.

## Implicit Evangelization

Everyone involved in faith-based reforms hopes that positive moral values and character traits will be transmitted, but conservative Christians seem to understand best how this will be accomplished, even when they are circumspect in their public pronouncements. Black evangelicals state forthrightly the linkage they see between church and community. But white evangelicals know liberals will be much more suspicious of their linking explicit Christian ideals to their outreach programs, so they are more careful in their public descriptions.

Privately, though, or among other evangelical Christians, white evangelicals make clear that they see in welfare reform a chance for churches to lead nonbelievers to Christ as they deliver social services or help in the community. They have no hope in "values in general," but they have great hope that the fruits of their efforts will convince others of the rightness of their position. They hope that as service recipients become involved with the Christian community, and as they eventually become Christians, the improvement in their lives will benefit them as individuals but also serve as a good example for the wider society.

This hope has led to an aggressive willingness on the part of faith-based reformers to push the envelope when possible. Each summer the mayor's office received grant proposals from various groups that sponsored summer programs for youth. During the early days of the Front Porch Alliance, this summer program became the Porchlight grant program. Faith-based groups were encouraged to apply. Those who read and refereed those proposals—and I was one— were encouraged to keep an open mind about faith-based experiments.

Because the Porchlight program was not funded by TANF, it did not fall under the new guidelines established by Charitable Choice. The money was to be dispersed with the clear understanding that it not be used for religious teaching or for any sectarian purpose. Inevitably, however, many of the grant proposals contained Bible study and other religious activities, because these were seen as integral to the kind of development children and teenagers in these programs would need. The mayor's office was clear that funded programs would have to be told that *no religious activity could occur during the portion of the daily routine that this money funded.* However, if these federal funds represented only three-fourths of the total program budget, then ostensibly biblical training or religious discussions could occur in the final two hours of the day if they had not occurred during the previous six. Routines could be designed so that the 9:00 A.M. to 3:00 P.M. portion was one program, paid for by federal funds and religious-content free, while the 3:00 P.M. to 5:00 P.M. portion was privately funded and available for religious activity. Children would not be required to attend the 3:00 to 5:00 portion, but they would be welcome to do so. Of course, the parents' typical workday made it likely that most children would attend both sessions.

Where federal strictures did not apply or where they were less clear, the mayor's representatives were more aggressive still. Like FPA, CHIP enlisted a group of local professionals to read and referee proposals for the Transitional Housing Program—and, again, I was one of these. Several of the readers balked at one particular proposal that included Bible study and explicit religious teaching. Not surprisingly, a representative from the Jewish Federation was especially concerned, but other liberals were worried as well that the programs not require recipients to become involved in explicitly Christian practice.

But the faith-based proponents were adamant. The money for the CHIP program came from the Lilly Endowment, albeit via the United Way of Central Indiana. It was not subject to federal guidelines on church and state. In a program clearly designed to enlist congregations as partners, it did not make sense, they argued, to prohibit those congregations from acting religiously. It was, after all, precisely the religious nature of this service provision that made it attractive and was, at the very least, the dependent variable in this demonstration program. If we wanted to learn whether faith-based groups could do a better job, why were we restricting their practice of faith?

The CHIP readers, however, were drawn mostly from the secular social service community and local government, and they tended to disagree. It was clear that they were not concerned only about breaking the law but also about linking service provision to religious content. In short, they thought it unfair that any potential client might be subjected to religious teaching against her will. Proponents argued, to no avail, that similar secular services existed and that the client could choose those, but the group opted against any very explicit religious content.

It is possible, of course, that other congregations that did receive funding have engaged in Bible study and religious teaching but were canny enough to keep those elements out of their proposal. No funding organization has sufficient monitoring and evaluative resources to police all such activity even if they had the will to do so. But the lines were drawn. Any group putting itself up for public funding, or even for foundation funding, had to learn to play the game. And playing the game meant a willingness to show that your efforts could not be viewed as unduly sectarian. Judge Payne, for his part, was openly willing to push the envelope. He openly encouraged his providers to teach spiritual values and welcomed any legal challenge. Like Mayor Goldsmith, he implied, "Sue me." Either man would likely have been happy to serve as the symbolic legal test case for faith-based practices.

In their desire to test the boundaries of legal changes, both Judge Payne and Mayor Goldsmith represented the evangelical desire to use public money for religious ends. Amy Sherman, a researcher who is also a ministry adviser to a Virginia congregation as well as to the Bush White House, put the matter most succinctly. In a public forum in Indianapolis on May 15, 1999, she said that the issue of religious content in social service was still undetermined. Charitable Choice made it clear that religious groups could still display symbols of their faith and could discriminate in their hiring, but they could not use the funding for explicitly sectarian or evangelistic practices. The courts had not yet determined the interpretation of those explicitly sectarian and evangelistic practices, but, she said, *"committed Christians should hope for a very broad interpretation."*

That hope embodies the evangelical position in faith-based reforms. For these evangelicals, good values and appropriate conduct are part of the same package as right belief and worship. Christians should maintain their goal of leading the lost to Jesus and should use these new resources at their disposal—whether from government or foundations—so long as their goal is not compromised.

Evangelicals can hardly be faulted for this tactic so long as they are clear about their purposes. It would be wrong to suggest that they were using the delivery of human services as some sort of cover for their underlying goal of evangelizing. It would be better to say that, for them, services and community development are about the whole person, and the whole person must be in right relationship to God through Jesus. Most evangelicals fully intend to use grant funds to deliver the services for which they contract and are willing to be evaluated on their outcomes, as would any group. But they are confident of producing positive outcomes because they believe that belief and practice are part of the same integrated package.

There is an uneasy alliance between religiously conservative reformers looking to stretch the guidelines governing their access to public or foundation funds and the liberal reformers who are looking at new ways to build stable communities capable of supporting the weakest members within them. Liberals want to make social services and community development more locally based and more customized to the clients who will be served. They see in congregations the hope for true local involvement. But what they are most likely to find are evangelicals, both black and white, who have their own goals and their own hopes about what the reforms will accomplish.

## Embedded in Community

Most reformers hope faith-based initiatives will lead to the transmission of positive social values. Some see those values as embedded in specific kinds of belief and practice that they hope to promote. A third, related hope for faith-based reform is that it will replace the simple provision of material support, case by case, with a true community of support that is sustaining and ongoing.

Marvin Olasky, one of the early leading lights of faith-based reforms, put the matter most clearly in a speech he delivered in Indianapolis in August 1998 at a Hudson Institute conference. Most of us, he suggested, have numerous support systems, some of which are deeply personal. When we are in trouble, we turn to our family and friends for support. The mere thought of turning to the government or to charity is dehumanizing and alienating for us. But the neediest individuals, and the most impoverished communities, seem to lack the network of support capable of bridging the gaps in their lives. There is a deep, persistent hope that communities of faith can become surrogate communities for those they serve, that they can essentially adopt the needy and go far beyond the simple provision of material support.

This was precisely the motivation behind Mississippi Governor Kirk Fordice's attempt to enlist congregations in his Faith and Families program. In 1994 he issued a challenge to the churches. If each church would help just one poor family reestablish itself, it could end welfare. As a result, many churches set out to become surrogate communities for those struggling to get by.

A number of other locales, including Indianapolis, tried to copy the Mississippi example. In Indianapolis, Mayor Goldsmith threw his support behind the local Faith and Families initiative spearheaded by a layman from one of the Lutheran churches. As in Mississippi, however, the concept of surrogate community foundered.

The Mississippi tale is well recounted in a 1996 article in *U.S. News and World Report* story entitled "Can Churches Save America?" (Shapiro 1996). The Mississippi churches found that the neediest cases needed far more than they could provide. The congregations imagined someone a little down on her luck who needed a hand with child care or better clothes to wear to an interview. What they found were people with a series of problems that could not be addressed simply or ad hoc. The *U.S. News* story recounts the experiences of one woman. Her slight economic rise, aided by the congregation, caused her to lose entitlements to a number of benefits. Moreover, the congregation was upset that it had invested $1,400, much more than it had intended.

Despite the small improvement in life for the client and the perceived magnitude of the sacrifice by the congregation, this case was seen as one of the few successes. At the 1996 writing, only 21 cases had moved off of welfare under the program in two years.

Congregations that volunteered for Faith and Families in Indianapolis experienced similar problems. Their stories help illuminate the difficulties inherent in trying to create surrogate communities. One of the most pressing problems is that the congregations most interested in serving this function, and the ones with the spare resources to do it, are made up of members from different class and racial backgrounds than the clients they would serve. In Indianapolis, the congregations who signed on for Faith and Families came from the middle and upper middle class. There were a couple of Catholic parishes and one synagogue, but by and large the churches came from the Protestant mainline.

It is highly unlikely in such a situation that a relationship of true community will occur between the congregations and their adopted families. Genuine friendships between individuals might certainly arise, but the gulf between the clients and the organizations remains considerable. Even when race is not a factor, class remains. The middle-class African-American churches most involved in new reforms serve a population of people much poorer than their members. I have already argued that African Americans are no more likely to live in the neighborhood where their church is located than are whites. They are also no more likely to share the class and status backgrounds of the people they serve.

Another factor militating against surrogate communities is age. In Indianapolis, the percentage of congregation members over the age of 55 is twice the percentage in the general population, a figure that corresponds to national averages. Not surprisingly, only half as many people between the ages of 19 and 35 are to be found in congregations as are in the population as a whole.

It is no criticism of congregations to say that their members are, on average, older, but it is a reality that must be considered. Many of the families in poverty are young, most often headed by single mothers. There is no reason to believe that elderly congregations cannot help these young families, but there are good reasons to imagine that such congregations may not function well as surrogate communities for them.

Differences in class, race, and age, coupled with the problems of multiple social disorders, combine to make things very difficult for congregations that hope to provide the comfortable bounds of community for people who desperately need a support network. Once one takes away the misconception that congregations are part of the local neighborhood with close personal connections, as discussed in Chapter 4, the ideal of a surrogate community becomes even more problematic.

## Positive Male Role Models

One very specific hope of faith-based reformers, linked to the idea of surrogate community, is that churches might provide some positive role models for adolescent males who most desperately need them. This hope is especially strong in the African-American community, where the proportion of families headed by single females in even higher than in the white community, where it is also alarmingly high.

The sponsors of new programs meant to involve the faith community make no secret of their hopes. Judge Payne saw his office facing a difficult problem. The majority of the juveniles sentenced in his court were African-American males. The majority of secular social workers attempting to address the needs of these children were white, middle-aged, usually female social workers.

African-American male leadership attempted to step up to the task. Martin University, an African-American institution in Indianapolis, established a program to provide counselors. Several churches or coalitions of churches established programs wherein their pastors would also become juvenile counselors. But as Chapter 4 highlighted, the road forward is rocky. There are administrative issues previously unexplored by the congregations. There is tension between secular social workers and pastors with very different training. There is also the uncomfortable demographic fact that the juveniles most in need of help seem to be young males, while the congregations themselves (if not their pastors) have high concentrations of older females.

The Front Porch Alliance also reached out to African-American pastors. The boldest effort of the FPA was an attempt to develop activism among the African-American pastors of Indianapolis on the model of the 10 Point Coalition led by Rev. Eugene Rivers in Boston. A former Harvard student, Rivers began an in-your-face street ministry as a Pentecostal pastor in the Boston inner city. He was soon joined by others, and they succeeded in drastically reducing the number of violent deaths in the city. Indeed, for a while there were no youth-on-youth murders on their watch.

At the invitation of Mayor Goldsmith, Rivers came to speak to a public meeting in Indianapolis. What many had imagined as a spirited pep talk was more spirited than they might have anticipated. Rivers castigated the African-American pastors for their lack of initiative. He berated them for their unwillingness to take their message out into the street. Finally, he stung them with the criticism that is seldom spoken by other African-American pastors in public: "You can preach to 1,000 women, but you cannot come out into the street to talk to one young man."

But Rivers knew, as did Mayor Goldsmith, that there is no hidden army of young, male African-American adults sitting in churches ready to be mobilized to serve youth. A small cadre of pastors has certainly been mobilized by the efforts of their peers and with the encouragement and support of local government. But their group is not the tip of a large iceberg, and anecdotes about their successes, accurate as they may be, should not be taken as leading indicators of much more to come.

This is not to say that women of any age, or older men, cannot help address the needs of adolescent males. But hopes that a great untapped resource lies just beneath the surface of the faith community should be tempered by demographic reality. At the very least, it would be asking a lot from a heroic group of male pastors.

The idea of transforming values, of imbuing people troubled by addictions or inadequate personal responsibility with the ethic of hard work, sobriety, thrift, and good parenting, is intuitively appealing. And there can be little question that changing lives is the business most congregations are in. It should not be too surprising, then, to find civic leaders, foundation officials, and other potential partners turning to congregations to help address the spiritual poverty, alongside the material poverty, of our needy fellow citizens.

But taken far beyond the "good idea" stage into practice, the initial appeal begins to wear thin. Congregations do not teach values "in general." What they do is theologically content-specific. Most people are happy to have congregations be as specific as they like with their own money but are unwilling to pay to see values they do not share, and especially values they openly oppose, be aggressively transferred to others.

So potential partners must either accept that congregations have specific beliefs and presuppositions and allow them to pursue these varied ends, or they must seek to block the very thing that differentiates congregations or other faith-based groups from any other kind of service provider. Indeed, given the problems congregations face administratively and financially, it is fair to say that the biggest advantage they offer as service providers is their commitment to specific beliefs and values. Without these, they are small organizations for whom social services are primarily secondary activities.

Here the specific cultural and theological ecology of a place becomes an important variable. Admittedly, there are few places left in America where no political and theological diversity exists, but some places are unarguably more diverse than others. What congregations can presume to teach, and what values and beliefs they can assume are shared by the large majority of the community, varies from place to place. It varies, in fact, from neighborhood to neighborhood, depending on just how racially, ethnically, or religiously homogeneous it is.

But even when homogeneity is great and diversity less of a concern, key demographic facts must temper our optimism about what congregations can do. Most congregations are, ultimately, collections of relatively similar people with shared interests. The better off they are, the more likely they are to have the resources necessary to serve the poor, but the less likely they are to be located near poor neighborhoods or to have anything in common with those they would serve. Therefore, the kind of congregations who join Faith and Families may try to become a surrogate family or community for the needy whose lives they touch, but very rarely do service recipients become colleagues or members.

Even more specific problems make this community building more difficult still. Congregational members are older, on average, than the general population, yet service recipients tend to be young families or unattached adolescents and young adults. African-American adolescent males are frequently the target for faith-based services, but the churches are filled with women who will not ultimately be the sought-after male role models.

Because this analysis sounds so dire, it is reasonable to ask: But don't congregations nonetheless help many people change their value systems and get on the right track? The answer, of course, is that they do. But congregations generally do this either by helping people much like themselves, people who can gradually join the community, or by offering services not so far different than what secular agencies provide. Congregations provide an enormous and previously underappreciated safety net for those not fully served by government or the secular nonprofit sector (Cnaan, Wineburg, and Boddie 2000), but that is different from the wholesale values change sought by many reformers.

# 7   What Happens to Congregations?

Government cannot be replaced by charities, but it can and should welcome them as partners. We must heed the growing consensus in America
that successful government social programs work in fruitful partnership with
community-serving and faith-based organizations—whether run by Methodists, Muslims, Mormons, or good people of no faith at all. (Bush 2001)

Various hopes and expectations attend the greater participation of congregations in public life. Many political leaders hope congregations can lead the effort
to privatize social services as much as possible. Some on the left use this as an
accusation to score points. They make the claim that conservative, usually Republican politicians are merely trying to reduce taxes and withdraw public support from the needy. But this view fails to recognize that President Clinton
signed the Charitable Choice legislation that President Bush hoped to expand
or that Clinton's Department of Housing and Urban Development first developed an office of faith-based initiatives.

It is easy to demagogue on this issue and to accuse reformers of ill intent. Yet
it is difficult to point to many actual politicians who make the strong argument
that government at all levels should abandon public social services and simply
let the churches, along with other private charities, take care of things. In most
quarters, there are reasoned arguments—and reasonable people can disagree—
over which services are best provided by private organizations and which by
public services. And even when one acknowledges that some things are best
handled at the public level, it is possible to disagree about whether local, state,
or federal public control makes the most sense (Lenkowsky 2001; Carlson-Theis
2000; Sherman 2000).

Most supporters of greater congregational involvement want to provide all
private groups with the opportunity to compete for public funds to provide
services. This is similar to the argument for competition between public and
private schools, an argument that often includes the idea of school vouchers.
But in this case, there is no union of social workers with strength anywhere near
that of the federal teacher's unions, so there is less organized resistance to experimentation with public and private mixtures.

Supporters want private groups like congregations to compete for government funds for the same reason any business or individual allows bids for any
service: they believe private groups can do a better job. As this book has attempted to show, they believe congregations and other private groups would

provide better services for a variety of reasons. Congregations would, they hope, have less bureaucratic overhead. Congregations are, they trust, more attuned to local needs. Congregations can, they assert, impart the necessary life skills and values that allow the needy to move beyond their poverty into self-sufficiency.

As this book has also attempted to show, the case of Indianapolis poses good questions to ask about all of these expectations. The case for privatization, and particularly the case for the benefits that would accrue from greater involvement by congregations, is not as strong as supporters sometimes suggest. Nonetheless, it is pointless to deny that in some circumstances congregational services seem to be the preferable option and that in virtually all cases congregations are already doing a great deal of work, even if haphazardly on an ad hoc basis, to provide an invisible safety net (Cnaan, Wineburg, and Boddie 2000). However, there are enough unanswered questions and enough limits to congregational capacity to insist that we move slowly in shifting what has been essentially public work toward the private sector.

One strong argument for pursuing these new partnerships, albeit cautiously, is that many congregations themselves want to be greater providers of services and want access to public funds for that purpose. This is especially true in the black community, where congregations are many times more likely to be receptive to government overtures and to the idea of using public funds to provide services. There is also a core group of white or interracial churches, predominantly downtown churches committed to what is commonly called urban ministry, who see this as an opportunity to reform welfare service delivery by tying financial aid to social and moral improvement.

In the best case, specific congregations will choose, without undue pressure or coercion, to join in partnerships with government, foundations, or private secular organizations. They will make those particular contributions for which they are best suited. They will receive a proportionate share of public funds, given the service they provide, and will fill gaps in the current social services environment. In that same best case, specific congregations will bring their knowledge of local culture, their understanding of ethnic or racial characteristics, and their desire to help others to bear on pressing social problems. They will work efficiently, especially with regard to limited bureaucracy, to get services to those who need them. They will recognize their limitations as organizations and work with other organizations to provide referrals and recommendations so clients can get the expertise they need.

In this ideal situation, congregations will go beyond the simple provision of services to help clients reconsider the behaviors that may contribute to their inability to become self-sufficient. By no means is poverty always a direct result of personal choices, but neither are the two always unrelated. In the best case, congregations will recognize where moral guidance would be effective and will provide it. They will help clients escape their substance abuse, gambling addictions, physical abuse, or inability to maintain a stable home environment. Furthermore, congregations will do this without alienating those with different

beliefs or separating social services into camps of people with different theological opinions.

Finally, in the best case, congregations will find this public role—new to
some, old hat to others—a good match for their other ministries. The tasks
they perform in the public sector will build communication between their own
members and the clients who may live in very different social worlds. The ministry they offer will edify their own members, not just the recipients of their
efforts. Parishioners will see themselves as contributing parts of a larger social whole whose job it is, not to do everything, but to do those things they can
do best.

## Potential Pitfalls

The best case outlined above is offered without sarcasm. Obviously,
no real-life scenario will match these expectations, but any endeavor must be
judged, even if judged charitably, by its own ideals. However, there are serious
obstacles between present reality and the admirable goals established by these
ideals. In our observations of emerging partnerships in Indianapolis, we have
noted several potential problems that congregations face as they enter into new
alliances. The chapters on subsidiarity, local knowledge, and the transmission
of values all offer general cautions to everyone interested in current changes to
public policy. They are meant to dampen enthusiasm and to lower the highest expectations about the capacity of congregations to effect sweeping social
changes. They show that while congregations can do some things, they cannot,
as an entire group of organizations, meet the highest expectations and assumptions now set before them. Given that, they also show that rushing toward even
greater privatization through congregational involvement is an exercise in poor
judgment.

How congregations will or will not be able to contribute to the common good
through these new partnerships is not, however, the only question worth asking.
Whatever congregations may be capable of, it is unfair to assume that they exist
solely for the purpose of serving the common good in whatever policy arrangements are deemed most efficient. Congregations have their own goals as organizations. They succeed as community-building organizations and as developers
of upstanding citizens, not to mention as the seedbed for so many who make
up the voluntary sector of our society, that it would be foolish not to take into
account their own organizational imperatives when considering the new partnerships (Etindi 1999; Sherman 1995; Jeavons and Cnaan 1997).

## Public Pressure

Congregations face many challenges as new changes take place. The first
is how they will respond to increased pressure from foundations and government officials to become more involved in civic life and to do more to provide

social services. Some will immediately respond that there is no real pressure from civic leaders. Congregations are free, after all, to choose whether or not to join in any new partnerships. The legal changes under Charitable Choice or under the proposals of the 2000 presidential candidates were meant only to make options available to congregations, not to force them in any way.

While it is certainly true that none of the legal changes forced congregations to do anything, it is also true that in Indianapolis we have seen considerable pressure exerted by civic leaders. At a presentation to Mayor Goldsmith and some of his top advisors, I made the argument that congregations were very independent, that they might be led in a certain direction but they would not be pushed. The mayor claimed that it was his cajoling, if not actual arm-twisting, of the senior pastor that prompted a large suburban church to open an inner-city recreation program as a mission outpost.

At another meeting, one of the mayor's aides lamented the fact that the congregations in inner-city black neighborhoods were lethargic. "The members drive in on Sunday," the aide said, "and then they drive out." She suggested in this large meeting that if those groups were threatened with the loss of their tax-exempt status, then maybe they would be more eager to provide social services to those who live around their church buildings. Others at the table played down that last suggestion, well aware that the mayor's office did not grant, nor could it rescind, the tax-exempt status of churches. But the philosophy behind the awkward suggestion was widely shared: congregations are supposed to serve the community, and their legal protections are linked to that obligation.

Congregations should consider carefully the ramifications of that assumption. Many who study the legal issues surrounding religion's role in society describe the tax-exempt status of churches as linked to separation of church and state, a principle that has evolved directly, though not unchallenged, from constitutional requirements concerning no establishment of religion. But many in the broader public see the favorable treatment of congregations as analogous to the treatment of other private charities: churches are really just charitable organizations with religious purposes; like other tax-exempt charities, their activities are subject to public scrutiny because the public grants them this exemption.

It would be wise not to infer too much from one incident, but the idea that churches owe something to their communities and have a moral obligation to provide services is not just anecdotal but widespread. It is worth repeating that fully 68 percent of those who are not congregational members think that social service should be these groups' highest priority. Civic leaders, especially neighborhood organizers, repeatedly bemoan the fact that the churches do not seem to do enough or that the churches spend all their money on themselves. Everyone knows that most churches provide some sort of service, even if only ad hoc, but this does not dampen the expectation that they could and should be doing more.

Linked to these assumptions is the idea that congregations have some large capacity that they are not tapping for the greater good. Many assume that congregations have money or volunteer time that they are hoarding. As described earlier, the fact that most congregations are stretched beyond their capacity does little to dispel the notion that they could do more if only they would.

As reforms move forward and new partnerships emerge, congregations must consider how they will respond to the expectation that they ought to do something—not only as a moral obligation, but as one tied to their legal standing as organizations. It is one thing to say that congregations have some theological obligation to help the poor—and it is clear that most congregants feel they have an obligation to do something—but it is another matter entirely for a broader public to think that congregations owe something to society and to have unrealistic expectations of them.

## Political, Geographic, and Theological Alliance

A second risk posed to congregations is that they will become competitors in a local neighborhood environment. Proponents of a greater public role for congregations are upbeat about the possibility of mixing congregations more effectively in the activities of community development centers, economic development campaigns, local health clinics, and the like. There are very good reasons to promote this sort of interaction, and at the broad level of the community, most people benefit from greater communication among individuals and organizations. That is why I have suggested the role of information gatekeepers in urban communities, a role that will be outlined further in the next chapter.

But for congregations, entering the world of community activism and economic development contains costs. In Indianapolis, as in other cities, there is keen competition among neighborhoods for limited public funds. When Mayor Goldsmith announced that the city had selected seven "target neighborhoods" that were earmarked for revitalization, there was considerable resentment on the part of neighborhoods that were not chosen. Once they enter the arena of grant competitions and public funding, congregations become players in a highly political process of building alliances with certain organizations and identifying other organizations or neighborhoods as the competition—if not, indeed, the enemy.

Even within neighborhoods there are clearly groups that work together and other groups that do not. Sometimes those boundaries are tied to long political histories. In other cases, where congregations are involved, there are genuine theological differences. It is well known in Indianapolis that one of the missions for homeless men is very conservative and evangelical. Men who go there know they will be required to read the Bible and listen to sermons in exchange for room and board. Conservative churches throughout the metropolitan area send money to that mission because it promotes theological views with which they agree. More liberal or mainline congregations, however, send their money, not to this ministry, but to a different one that takes an approach its supporters would define as more open-minded. The donor lists for these groups are almost completely different.

The difficulties posed by this sort of theological segregation will be apparent. These missions, like all organizations, are located in specific places. But even within their own neighborhoods, not all of the other service organizations or congregations wish to work cooperatively with them and would assume considerable risk through cooperation even if they wished to do so. The mainline congregations, especially, risk being tainted as potential partners if they cooperate too closely with an evangelical mission that is perceived to be insensitive or bullying with its clients.

In another case, a very large Missionary Baptist congregation on the east side applied for funds from CHIP to convert vacant public housing into transitional homes for the homeless. They decided, for a variety of political and theological reasons, to do this with a ministerial alliance doing community development on the west side. This raised the hackles of other eastside groups that could not help but feel that their expertise had been slighted.

It would be misleading to overstate the degree of division here. It is not as if Indianapolis social services are balkanized into competing camps that are always at each others' throats. But it is clearly true that in the competition for scarce resources, the participants form alliances that are political, geographic, and theological. Every organization has peculiar interests that favor certain political, geographic, and theological tendencies, though these may be stronger or weaker in any individual case. Unfortunately, the three do not always line up neatly, so organizations must decide where their greatest interests lie.

Every group mentioned above would likely say that it did not see itself in direct competition with the others. Every individual involved would say that she or he only wanted what was best for the community. Although both of these statements would be true, they would mask the underlying, inevitable competition that characterizes public or philanthropic funding. It is the nature of life that choices are complex and that more than one thing can be true at the same time. But congregations entering into partnerships with secular charities, community groups, foundations, and government must think clearly about their priorities. They must consider their political, geographic, and theological priorities and be prepared to compete for their interests.

This competitive model is new for most congregations and poses a variety of risks. Who will decide for the group? What role will clerical leadership play in political or civic decisions? What is the group's level of commitment to the local neighborhood, and what happens when other organizations in the neighborhood make choices that are theologically or politically unappealing?

The point is not, surely, that congregations should avoid community or economic development because they might get their hands dirty. The point is rather that they should both be prepared to get their hands dirty and look ahead clear-sightedly toward the decisions they will make.

## Evangelizing and Proselytizing

One of the greatest hopes of those arguing for a broader role for religious organizations in social services and community development is that religious service providers will be able to instill values alongside the delivery of needed services. As noted in Chapter 6, this is not done as easily or as often as proponents might hope. Civil libertarians are quick to note the risks to service recipients. They have justifiable concerns about whether clients can receive services free from sectarian religious sentiment, if that is what the clients wish.

But the belief that congregations can instill values and teach proper belief poses considerable risks to congregations themselves. Most congregations promote particular beliefs and values as a matter of course. Some are aggressively evangelical as they communicate these beliefs to others. Some are more quiet but still clear in their convictions.

When congregations accept this role as part of a larger partnership, however, they open themselves to unimagined challenges. Civic leaders hope that congregations can instill positive moral values such as hard work, frugality, chastity, and sobriety. What they sometimes do not understand is that congregations do not promote these values in and of themselves. Moral values and moral practice are grounded in a worldview that is highly theological. Most religious adherents do good as part of an entire philosophy of life that is, at its core, a statement of how the world really is. For example, for a large segment of Christianity, right action is, in and of itself, not the central issue. If one is not converted, if one does not accept Jesus Christ as personal Lord and Savior, then all the good acts and appropriate moral behavior in the world will not affect one's eternal salvation.

Congregations must prepare for inevitable challenges to the specific theological content of their ministries. They will either have to abandon Bible study, evangelization, and proselytization; downplay these in their public presentations; or confidently assert that they know best and prepare for the challenges—including lawsuits—that will inevitably follow. The rhetoric of faith-based reforms is that we must judge these efforts by their outcomes; the reality is that the methods used will be under constant public scrutiny if public funds are in play.

## Professionalization of Congregational Ministries

One very specific internal risk faced by congregations who become partners with government or foundations is that the nature of their ministries will change. There is a pressing concern, to which we will return, that funding rules and regulations will interfere with a congregation's ability to order its own ministries. But there is a more acute danger that even without such formal restriction, congregations will alter how they do business to accommodate their new roles as public partners. The most obvious form of this accommodation is professionalization. Congregations may begin their inquiries into new partnerships via their pastor or some mission subcommittee. But any congregation that spends much time in this arena eventually considers hiring a professional staff member to be responsible for community ministries.

Typical is the case of an urban Presbyterian congregation with a longtime commitment to urban ministry. The group has fewer than one hundred members, and about forty are present on any given Sunday morning. Those forty account for an annual budget of around $40,000. Yet the congregation has, in the recent past, maintained urban mission programs costing in excess of $100,000. They did this through partnership with a much larger suburban Presbyterian church that supported them as an urban mission, but also through government grants to support job training for youth. As this congregation considered its role in the Front Porch Alliance and in other emerging partnerships, it realized that its administrative needs had far exceeded its staff's capacities. They began writing a grant to supply sufficient funds to hire a part-time grant writer in the hopes that such a person could eventually bring in enough funds, plus overhead, to fund her own salary.

As some congregations take on a new organizational focus in partnership with other different organizations, it is natural that they should incur start-up costs. At the least, they will need additional clerical help or office supplies. At the other extreme, they may need full-time program managers or grant writers. This is a cost that must be considered by funders, who must know that congregations do not have spare capacity and will need additional overhead funds in the short run. But it is a cost that must also be considered by congregations, who could change the nature of their ministries without knowing it.

Some congregations that have hired professional community ministers note a drop-off in volunteer time spent on those ministries. When so much is needed, it is easy to say, "Well, we've paid to have that taken care of, so we can turn our attention to something else." Not only is this frequently not true—as new professional staff members find themselves faced with tasks previously done by dozens of volunteers—but it changes the relationship between the congregation and its ministry. The soup kitchen or homeless shelter may still be a funded mission of the group, but it has ceased to be a group activity that is community-building and mission-reinforcing in and of itself.

It is easy to lay guilt at the feet of congregations for merely spending their money on the poor rather than spending time with them, but the question need not be one of moral worth. Whatever the moral difference between funding a professionally delivered program and taking part in one as a community of participating volunteers, the practical difference is that the latter builds community and continually models the beliefs and behaviors that the group promotes.

This is one of the reasons that a project like Habitat for Humanity is so popular with congregations. Those in the professional service world often sneer, in private, at programs like Habitat because they require so little commitment from the congregations that get involved. The projects last just a day or two, and the congregants can walk away self-satisfied, having made no effort to change the structural elements that lead to housing problems and having had no real contact with the needy who stand to benefit.

Admittedly, the lack of any formal, long-term commitment is attractive to some congregations. They are not sure their budget will cover their expenses for this year, much less for next year or the year after that. Moreover, their own building is likely to be in need of substantial repairs that may require yet another mortgage.

But another attraction of programs like Habitat is that they are concrete, substantial opportunities for members of the community to work together toward a deliverable product. The members can look at one another and say, "We did that together." The same community-building spirit is not available in the act of paying a professional to deliver a ministry.

The reverse of that problem is, of course, that congregations that are able to write grants and who have professional staff members with the time and responsibility for delivering community ministries are also likely to be the most successful in grant competitions and to get the most done. In Mapleton-Fall Creek, for instance, the churches that have had full-time community ministers have undoubtedly made the closest connections to the neighbors. Although problems of race and culture still exist for these middle-class, mainline groups seeking to minister to their mostly black, mostly poor neighbors, only professional staff—or full-time volunteers, a rare commodity—are able to spend the hours, weeks, and years needed to establish trust and communication.

Despite the grumbling when the large Baptist church turned to partners outside the neighborhood, the fact remained—and the funding committee recognized it—that this church would be able to devote an associate minister as a full-time project manager to this project. Whatever other community-based problems might arise, this church would not have to face the biggest problem encountered by most proposed congregational endeavors: it had the resources to get the ball rolling. Nonprofit organizations entering into partnership with congregations want to see positive results for the money they spend. They want to show their funders that they chose wisely. Therefore, experimental partnerships are likely to choose congregations that can dedicate professional staff to the project at hand, despite the fact that such congregations are relatively few and far between.

Congregations that consider partnership with foundations and government are faced with a choice. They can rely on their pastor and on volunteers, but they may soon find themselves well out of their depth, and they are likely, in any event, to be at a disadvantage in competition for funds. They can add professional staff, but this is likely to alter the community-building nature of their missions. They must decide what level of commitment they want to make—and perhaps most importantly, what results they hope to achieve.

The head of an inner-city youth program, himself a professional urban missionary paid by a large suburban church, made his own decision clear. "My goal," he said, "is to minister to the members of my congregation by providing this mission opportunity to enhance their spiritual growth. No matter how much good we do in the community where our program is, if it is not an opportunity for our own members to grow, then we've failed."

## Institutional Isomorphism

Our research team made a public presentation to a group of young civic leaders drawn together by the Chamber of Commerce. We were describing some of the new social welfare initiatives in which congregations were serving as partners. As soon as we had finished, one of the participants raised her hand. "I want to know," she said, "if congregations become social workers, who will do what they used to do?"

There are two sets of issues bound up in that one concise question. The first issue is one that only congregations can answer for themselves: Can congregations become more involved in public partnerships, can they become part of the community development and social service community, without detriment to their other core missions such as preaching and teaching?

Some large congregations are obviously able to manage many mission activities at once. They have professional staff for preaching, moral education, counseling, and a variety of missions ranging from recreation to what is traditionally called urban ministry. But most congregations are relatively small and have only one full-time staff member. The degree to which they can become involved in such partnerships and still maintain their other ministries is for them to decide.

If the reports of urban pastors are any indication, most congregations make their opinions on this issue clear. Most pastors will tell you that as long as they preach well and visit the sick and elderly, they can get involved in political or civic or neighborhood activities. But if their preaching or visitation slips, the congregation will be there to remind them who pays the bills and what services they require. Some congregations, obviously, have made the decision to make urban ministry the focus of their missions. But for most, it is a part of a much larger package, and the day-to-day parts of that package are that their traditional needs for worship, religious education, and visitation be met.

But there is a second set of issues involved in the question, "Who will do what they used to do?" Even if congregations can still get the preaching and visitation done, there is still a concern that their core values, their theological and even prophetic principles, can be compromised by entrance into these partnerships.

The most explicit version of this concern is that congregations, like any organization, will eventually come to embody the values and practices of the larger institutions that support it. Catholic parishes, for instance, differ on many details, depending on the details of their local environment and on the priest himself. But as a set of organizations, parishes are influenced by policies set in their diocese, their archdiocese, and even in Rome. Priests who wish to move up the ecclesiastical ladder and congregations that seek support from the larger bodies learn to behave in ways that conform to the institution's standards.

Sociologists call this process *institutional isomorphism,* but the phenomenon is easy enough to understand. The big institutions that provide funds set certain standards. They see programs that deliver the desired results and name these as "best practices." Organizations that hope to get funded strive to live up to those standards and to institute those best practices to establish their worth (Milofsky 1997; Dimaggio and Powell 1991; Demerath et al. 1992). Over time, the entire field of organizations comes to look much the same. At some very basic level, they assume the core values of the organizations that provide the funding. So, for instance, juvenile social workers come to look very much alike because each looked around and saw what kinds of behaviors got funded and what kinds did not.

Congregations face the very real risk that they will subtly, even invisibly, come to embody values that help them succeed in the secular funding arena. This is not necessarily a problem in and of itself, but the risk remains that those secular funding values will run counter to values held by the congregation at the outset.

It is not special criticism of congregations to say that they may be forced to make certain compromises in order to get along in a partnership that involves organizations with different theologies or with no theologies at all. Each of us as individuals, and virtually all organizations, choose daily between our highest ideals and the realities of getting the job done in a world full of others with their own ideals. But congregations must be alert to the risks that they shift their practices, not because of shifts in their core beliefs, but because of needs expressed by funders in foundations or government.

## Regulation and Autonomy

The most important subset of the risk of isomorphism, and the one that has garnered the most attention, is the risk that involvement with government will eventually entail limitations and regulations on congregations' activities. If this occurred, it would not be the first time that government control had changed an institution's priorities. Of course, no congregation or denomination can be unaware of these risks. They can, however, be sanguine about how they will handle the situations. Most congregations are very confident that they will establish their mission thrust and, should government policy interfere with their theological decisions, they will simply stop taking the government's money.

I heard exactly that opinion expressed during a panel discussion between Amy Sherman and me. She expressed confidence that her congregation was committed to running its program as it saw fit. So long as federal funding was available to do that, they would take advantage of it. But should federal funding make requirements of them that they thought were contrary to their beliefs and intentions, then they would give back their public funding and carry forward with the program on their own.

Such sentiment is admirable, and there is little question that her congregation had the resources to carry through on its pledge. But many of the congregations entering new partnerships and coalitions operate on shoestring budgets. This is not simply a case of government channeling funds through existing, established programs as alternatives to public programs. In many cases, the partnerships are creating new programs, made out of whole cloth, whose sole source of funding is the new arrangement.

While it is noble enough for congregations to say that they will stick to their theological principles and refuse the government funding if unacceptable strings are attached, it is easy to envision a situation where this will be easier said than done. One can easily imagine a congregational program that pays, say, two professional ministers who are the sole support of their families. Further, let us imagine that such a program also provides services for two dozen families headed by single women. All of the funding for this program comes through a partnership with government.

Now imagine a legal change whereby a new law states that no federally funded program can deny women the right to use their vouchers or stipend to obtain an abortion. Many evangelical churches would surely want to withdraw from any connection with such funding, but is the church in question willing to put the families of two ministers as well as the families of twenty-four women clients at risk? It is easy enough to say that principles will come first or that the congregation will find alternative funding elsewhere, but who can say what will happen when the rubber hits the road?

Although congregations, like all organizations, have their own internal politics, they are usually immune from the direct pressures created by legal changes and funding requirements. In the new coalitions and partnerships, they will have to take the possibility of changing mandates and standards into account. Under Charitable Choice, congregations are allowed to receive federal funds even if they choose to discriminate, for religious reasons, in their hiring, and even if they promote religion through the use of symbols. But they are not allowed to evangelize and proselytize.

What constitutes proselytization or evangelization—essentially, what counts and what does not under Charitable Choice—has not been determined in court. Some have advocated that Christians press for a broad interpretation so that they can share Christ with those they would serve. Others, and especially those from minority groups such as the Jewish Federation, will continue to argue that federal funding must include restrictive, constructive guides to sectarian practice.

Congregations must be aware that the guidelines and restrictions placed on them by the acceptance of public funding are malleable. If those restrictions change next year or in the next administration, congregations must be prepared either to change with them or to refuse the funds. Insofar as they establish new programs dependent on those funds, then they put themselves at risk of a serious dilemma.

# 8   Crossing Boundaries Cautiously

> The churches and synagogues of America can no more be omitted from responsible social analysis than can big labor, business corporations, or the communications media. Not only are religious institutions significant "players" in the public realm, but they are singularly important to the way people order their lives and values at the most local and concrete levels of their existence. Thus they are crucial to understanding the family, neighborhood, and other mediating structures of empowerment. (Berger and Neuhaus 1977)

Most of this book has been intentionally very cautionary because as I observed emerging partnerships among congregations and other organizations in Indianapolis, I was struck by the degree to which reality falls far behind the high expectations many bring to these new endeavors. The same might be said, of course, for any new venture. But there are real risks in assuming that congregations can do more than they actually are able to do in delivering social services or in spurring community development. The limitations on the capacity of congregations to do this sort of work must be recognized, and social policy made accordingly.

As Chapter 7 pointed out, the risks are not only to the recipients of services or to the existing service community but to the partner congregations as well. There is a major institutional shift occurring in America, and it will have profound consequences for all the organizations involved. Failure to contemplate the consequences, even though they can never fully be foreseen in advance, could be catastrophic. Moreover, the consequences must be considered at several different levels: the intended recipients, the congregations receiving new funding, and the organizational ecology of the community, which will need to achieve a new balance.

Given the many risks and cautions enumerated here, however, it is important to acknowledge that new partnerships with congregations will continue to evolve. Congregations do have unique contributions to make. They are often the organizations with the longest history in any given neighborhood. They are capable of mobilizing volunteer effort, and they have been in the business of promoting values and helping others for decades and even, in some cases, for centuries. That policy makers and philanthropists want the community to benefit from those gifts is only natural.

As those from local government and foundations consider the new partnerships they wish to encourage or to nurture, they should consider both the current state of community development and the special needs of congregations.

That is, they should attempt to see congregations in the context of the best available thinking about what communities, and the neediest individuals within them, most need.

## The Current Community Development Environment

This book has repeatedly noted the drive toward new social partnerships involving congregations and other religious organizations with traditional social service or community development organizations. The twin concepts of *partnership* and *social capital* energize Indianapolis's community planning. In city government and in foundations, proposals that involve a variety of individuals and organizations move to the top of the list. Proposals that involve the faith community in those partnerships are held in highest esteem, as the many examples in this book have recounted (Putnam 1995a and b; DiIulio 1997a; Koch and Johnson 1997; Messer 1998; Wolpert 1997).

The Lilly Endowment is funding local demonstration projects that mix government, traditional nonprofit service groups, and religious congregations. In the former Goldsmith administration, city hall, through which federal money passes in the form of Community Development Block Grants, tried to build cooperation and cross-programming among the various organizations, especially congregations, in urban neighborhoods. Both of these efforts mirror the national effort by HUD to encourage congregations to get involved in community development. They foreshadowed the even larger changes proposed by the Bush administration.

There is relatively little rhetoric in Indianapolis (or elsewhere) about government turning over full responsibility for social services to the churches and other private providers. But given the fact that the welfare rolls are reputed to be the smallest in thirty years, there is correspondingly little doubt that reform will continue and that private providers, including religious ones, will be shouldering a greater share of responsibility for welfare services and community development in the future. Everyone seems to recognize that what will emerge from today's experimentation and occasional confusion will be a mixed bag of public and private, sacred and secular.

The faith-based initiatives started in Indianapolis shared an assumption that faith-based organizations, especially congregations, added something important to service delivery. Each of the initiatives was based on partnership, whether with the city, the court, or private nonprofit groups. None naively assumed that religious groups could do the work on their own, but each believed that religious groups would bring something new to the table.

That "something new" was partnership's twin, *social capital*. These new partnerships, like the HUD initiative, were premised on the idea that congregations have both specific local knowledge and an ability to transmit and nurture values that secular organizations, whether public or private, lack.

This turn toward congregations flows from concrete changes in attitudes toward social service delivery. What needy people really need, so the new argument goes, is not merely money but hope, trust, discipline, and networks of support. As a report of the Urban Institute put it:

> Probably the feature that most starkly contrasts community building with approaches to poverty alleviation that have been typical in America over the past half-century is that its primary aim is not simply giving more money, services or other material benefits to the poor. . . . [The] central theme is to obliterate feelings of dependency and to replace them with feelings of self-reliance, self-confidence, and responsibility. (Gibson, Kingsley, and McNeely 1997)

Community building and community development have replaced more individualistic approaches to welfare. In Indianapolis, at least, the bulk of community development funding has been targeted at specific neighborhoods with the goal of building community there. Mayor Goldsmith's "Building Better Neighborhoods" initiative spanned the city, but the seven "target" neighborhoods were all in the inner city. Most of the funding, including the pass-through money from HUD that goes to social service groups and community development corporations, goes to organizations with specific geographic boundaries. Indeed, in a city with many fewer identifiable ethnic neighborhoods than places like Chicago, it is not too strong to say that the funding stream flowing through community development corporations and community centers has literally *created* neighborhood boundaries in Indianapolis.

Community building is a key feature in this way of thinking, and both city governments and major foundations are treating congregations as community-building institutions par excellence. More than a few religion scholars, including people like Nancy Ammerman and Donald Miller, have forwarded the Tocquevillian argument that congregations, as a special type of voluntary association, are premier generators of social capital in our society (Ammerman 1997; Orr et al. 1994; Milofsky 1997).

There are good reasons to wonder whether congregations really generate social capital or, perhaps better put, whether we need to be more precise about what social capital means. That congregations provide networks of support for, and teach important citizenship values and skills to, their members, as Ammerman has suggested, cannot be gainsaid. Congregations are often effective at building internal community. All of society benefits from having members of these communities as fellow citizens. Many studies have suggested that they are healthier, better adjusted, and less likely to need public help when times get tough.

But the sort of social capital that Robert Putnam has put on everyone's agenda is really not about the enduring strength of social enclaves and deep socialization. Putnam's thrust is toward a broader, more general sense of social trust and mutual obligation, something that must be thought of as *public* or *civic*. It is not nearly so clear that congregations offer this to any greater degree than other organizations. In fact, given the racial, class, and ethnic homogeneity exhibited by most congregations, there are good reasons to think that congregations do this less well than other groups.

In Indianapolis, the mayor, the judge, and the Lilly Endowment all sought pragmatic goals only indirectly connected to such social theory. They tried to link people who need help with stable, caring institutions. It is reasonable—indeed, nearly obligatory—for these service "payers" to assert that what juvenile delinquents or homeless persons or single moms really need are not a few additional services, but a supportive community. And it is reasonable, given current trends, for these groups to look to congregations to provide such communities. But there is virtually no evidence to suggest that the people being served by congregations are likely to become members of those congregational communities. One might hope that some of the religious and ethical values of the providing congregations rub off on the recipients, but the recipients do not see this provision of services as an invitation to join. More to the point, the congregations that are writing these new grant proposals and providing these services generally see this as a mission activity rather than as a method of recruitment.

Assumptions about congregations as supportive, value-filled communities are only one side of the social capital grail that lures community leaders. At least as important is the assumption that congregations are genuinely local organizations. Prevailing wisdom says that congregations are more "on the ground" than other organizations, that they are part of the neighborhood community and know local residents and their needs in ways that secular service groups cannot. If congregations are authentically indigenous organizations, then it makes sense to think that they must play a part in neighborhood community building. But as Chapter 4 argued, not all congregations are closely tied to their local neighborhoods.

Despite where members actually live, however, some congregations do have deep historical and social ties to the neighborhoods where their house of worship is located. Furthermore, those congregations that are providing social services to nonmembers or working on community development are likely doing so around the church or synagogue building.

Government entities, secular and religious service groups, and congregations themselves are each seeking to build partnerships because they want to leverage resources. The whole point of efforts such as the Front Porch Alliance (FPA) or the CHIP initiative to engage congregations as partners is to bring together groups with different talents and resources and to combine their efforts for maximum efficiency. The reasonable fear for all of these groups is that lack of coordination and the failure to form partnerships has led to duplication of services and inefficient use of money and time.

## Information as the Key to Successful Partnerships

Given this fear, it is telling that the resource most easily but least frequently leveraged is information. It may be impossible and ultimately self-defeating to try to coordinate closely the complex web of public, private secular, and private religious community development and service delivery. But it would be a much simpler matter to try to coordinate information so that groups could make their own choices and forward their own agendas with fuller knowledge of what is going on around them.

The kind of information needed has everything to do with understanding the local social ecology, but it is unhelpful to get bogged down in social scientific terminology. The majority of congregations simply lack even the most basic information they would need to be contributing partners in urban development. As the FPA tried earnestly to encourage congregations to apply for public and private funding for service and development, it became clear that most congregations knew nothing about the details that are second nature to other organizations that depend on external funding. Most congregations know little about how government works, how grants and contracts are awarded, or how human service programs are administrated and evaluated.

In truth, most congregations do not even know much about how other congregations work. Recall the study of congregations providing youth programming to nonmember children in which 80 percent of the program directors thought their programs were unique even though there were many other programs very similar to their own. Even among those who knew of other programs, only a couple could provide any details about other programs' size or direction.

Beyond this, most congregations know very little about the demographics of their neighborhood or about the secular service organizations that inhabit it. They do not see themselves as partners in a common enterprise, except in those isolated but growing instances when they are directly labeled partners in some new funding initiative. As little as some people in the faith community may know about government and about the social welfare bureaucracy, people in that bureaucracy often know less about the distinctiveness of faith communities.

In this new learning process, congregations seem to function best if they have some sort of community minister—a staff member whose full-time job it is to keep the congregation connected to the neighborhood, to city government, and to parachurch activities. Of course, few congregations can possibly afford such a full-time professional. In lieu of such a person, congregations seem best able to enter fruitful partnerships when they are connected to some other person or organization, frequently within their own neighborhood, who can provide that community link for them.

Money and technical ability, such as grant writing or program evaluation, may always be in short supply. But there is a significant gap between what congregations who would be partners know and what they need to know about grant writing, local government, program administration, evaluation, and the range of programming already available in the secular community.

This ignorance is not, one should hasten to add, entirely congregations' fault. Many of the people and organizations in the best position to provide this information have either steered clear of congregations or have not familiarized themselves with what congregations need in order to build useful partnerships. To some extent, those who have the information must make a conscious effort to approach congregations and to tailor information to their needs. Misinformation about what congregations do as well as lingering fears of illegal church-state partnerships conspire to keep congregations on the fringes of the public center.

But congregations are not blameless either. For a variety of reasons, many congregations have failed to build relationships with those right outside their door who can help them to understand the local environment and to navigate the often-mysterious world of grants, contracts, administration, and evaluation.

That is why I have suggested the notion of information gatekeeper. Some neighborhoods in Indianapolis have informal, often self-selected, local information gatekeepers, people who are "hooked up" to city government, to foundations, to local neighborhood efforts, and the like. Frequently these folks are the heads of community centers, whether faith-based or secular. Sometimes these people are the heads of community development corporations. Occasionally these people are precisely those "community ministers" who are staff members of better-off congregations.

When these information gatekeepers exist, they can be important catalysts for either inclusion or exclusion. They can help new leaders in urban communities where leadership turnover is high become acquainted with the local circumstances. They can, of course, also construct obstacles that ensure that certain people or groups never get involved.

Despite the fact that most neighborhoods have such gatekeepers, most congregations are unable to take full advantage of their knowledge and so never enjoy the leverage that these individuals provide. Knowledge has to be continually reproduced, with someone in each congregation needing to find out for him- or herself. There are several factors that help explain why congregations are unable to take advantage of the knowledge possessed by the relevant gatekeepers.

1. *The gatekeepers do not know anything about congregations.* Too often, the sort of people who run community centers or community development corporations know very little about the religious organizations in their own neighborhoods. Most Americans have only a hazy idea of how religious traditions other than their own operate. Finding out about religious groups—how they think, how leadership works, how decisions are made—is seldom part of the secular training done for city planners or nonprofit managers. Consequently, many of the people in these positions of neighborhood leadership view the churches or synagogues around them as black boxes. When people in government or nonprofit leadership complain that "the churches here don't do anything," they may be right—or they may simply have no idea of what the congregations really do or why.

If congregations are to be helpful partners in the new mix of public and private, sacred and secular, then training for nonprofit leaders must include significantly better information about faith traditions and about congregational polity. It is not enough, nor was it ever enough, to learn about theological differences among Protestants, Catholics, and Jews. Community leaders need to know something about the dynamics of parishes, tall-steeple churches, synagogues, and storefront chapels as *organizations.* Considerable research is being done in this area; nonprofit leaders must place this field on their intellectual horizon.

2. *The congregations do not know anything about the gatekeepers.* The shoe fits even more snugly on the other foot. While some neighborhood information gatekeepers do know something about congregations, and some are pastors or former pastors themselves, leaders in congregations, especially pastors, typically know nothing about local community-building organizations. Most clergy are taught nothing in seminary about how a neighborhood works or how nonprofit organizations contribute to community life. If a congregation has a community minister or an especially tuned-in layperson, its prospects are greatly improved, but few congregations have such resources.

3. *The "system" is not designed to cause overlap.* Social service professionals look to one another and to funders in government or in the nonprofit world as they model their activities. People in congregations frequently look toward their denomination or to others who share their theological beliefs for guidance and support. Community gatekeepers are usually tied, at least indirectly, to city government or to some kind of funding coalition. Even within the largest community funding agencies—in our city, the Lilly Endowment is paramount—the people who fund religious activities are different from those who fund community programming. There are few professional activities that build networking or information sharing across organizational and institutional lines. This is somewhat true within religious groups—Baptists do not share information well with Catholics—but it is even more true among and between different spheres of activity.

The operational dictum here is clear: information follows money. The sources of funding, including city government and private foundations, are loosening the information dams by insisting that some formerly secular initiatives begin to include partners from the faith community. They must now make it as possible as it is necessary for leaders in public or secular community work to learn about what the faith community brings to the table.

4. *Congregations insist on looking for faith-based information and models.* An especially important subset of factor three is the tendency for congregations and other faith-based nonprofits to want to circumscribe their efforts within the faith community. For example, many in the faith community repeatedly call for a directory of social services and community-building efforts undertaken by congregations—as if only things done by churches and synagogues would be useful to know about. It makes much more sense to look for partnerships and alliances that cut across interests and organizational boundaries than it does to

always think entirely inside the box and insist that only activities in very similar organizations matter.

Those congregational and denominational leaders who wish to participate in the emerging partnerships must learn about the world of city government and foundations, just as governmental and private funders must encourage grant recipients to learn about the faith community. To be sure, busy people are already inundated with more information than they can manage. But the risks associated with not knowing what else is happening as one seeks to develop programs is worse than the risk of information overload. The need to disseminate information effectively is yet another reason to turn to information gatekeepers.

5. *The information available is idiosyncratic.* Common to congregations, nonprofits, neighborhood leadership, and government is the problem that much necessary information is isolated and is frequently difficult to obtain. Consequently, congregations either find themselves faced with much too much information or much too little. Without a common source of data provided by someone who understands what each of these groups needs to know, it is difficult for anyone to serve the information processing function.

6. *Leaders are unable to analyze and interpret information.* Unfortunately, even the neighborhood information gatekeepers are not always good at understanding the data that comes before them, if by data one means important statistics or other kinds of quantifiable information. On the other hand, the gatekeepers usually do know the kind of programmatic information—who has Requests for Proposals outstanding, what those funders are really looking for, what other funding opportunities might be available, who is already providing similar services—that local congregations might take advantage of. Any weakness in data management or interpretation at the governmental level is magnified at the level of nonprofit management and then magnified again in congregational leadership.

7. *There is insufficient overlap and redundancy among gatekeepers.* No solitary person can or should serve as the information gatekeeper with connections to city government, local information providers (such as the universities), and the foundations. Each neighborhood must have multiple information gatekeepers, although ideally there must be a manageable number and the same information must be made available to them all. Even with this overlap, there will be opportunities for power struggles and exclusion as well as problems caused by turnover. But maintaining sufficient redundancy narrows these risks considerably.

8. *Leaders come and go.* Leaders of urban nonprofits or service groups change jobs frequently. So do urban pastors. While there is turnover in any environment, urban areas are especially affected by rapid turnover in all of the different organizations. Not only does this create stress (which contributes to the turnover), but it creates difficulty in maintaining an information stream within any given organization, much less between and among them.

Until congregations learn how to write grants, how federal HUD dollars are passed through the city and into the neighborhoods, how foundations solicit and fund proposals, and how secular service agencies staffed by social work professionals operate, they will never be effective partners in service delivery or community development. Even if congregations learn more about the social service world, their usefulness as partners will be limited until service and governmental professionals learn some basic information about religious organizations. Finally, both groups need to share common information about the environments they serve. Good demographic and programmatic information should be ground zero from which all the work of partnership begins.

This is not to say that demographic and programmatic information must always shape mission. Each group—and congregations most of all—must determine its mission *as an internal matter* and bring that mission to the table. But the effort to find coordination or cooperation among those missions begins with information.

There is an important, well-grounded fear that this sharing of information and better mutual understanding will gradually blur the organizational distinctions that are so important. By the phenomenon described in Chapter 7 as *institutional isomorphism,* organizations gradually come to model the expectations of funders, which is to say that they eventually all end up looking more or less like the groups who are most successful at fund-raising. This threat should not be taken lightly. Although it is generally good both to learn from others' mistakes and to reproduce successful programs, it is reasonable to think that increased overlap among different kinds of organizations will limit innovation. What is thought to be different or most valuable about congregations, for instance, may gradually fade.

The possibility of such a trend points to a potentially greater threat, which is that congregations compromise their ability to carry out their other forms of ministry. To put it simply, time and energy spent on learning about service and development, or in workshops on writing grants or evaluating programs, is time and energy not spent on worship or teaching. Insofar as congregations have excess capacity, this is not a problem. But do they?

A primary goal of government and foundations must be to make the necessary information available to all potential partners in ways that cost those partners as little time and energy as is possible. Coerced coordination of efforts, whether with carrots or sticks, will ultimately be destructive. Organizations of all kinds might eventually become something they had not meant to be.

Organizations must be allowed to form their own complex webs of partnerships and interactions, negotiating roles as they go in accordance both with the perceived need for service and with the organizations' own perceptions of their distinct missions. However, these partnerships and interactions will be more fruitful and less duplicative to the degree to that relevant information is available and transparent. Toward that end, public and private community leadership would do well to pursue four related goals for developing a productive information environment:

1. Baseline information about the community should be readily available and easily managed. Every organization that is a potential partner in neighborhood development, for example, should have access to census information, housing statistics, existing programs, and other relevant data. Collecting, managing, and then publicizing such information is expensive, especially at the outset. But in the long run, the inefficiencies associated with poor information and duplicated programs are much more expensive.

2. Leaders in government and community organizations should receive training about the dynamics of congregations and faith-based nonprofits. If the future holds complex new arrangements that mix private and public, sacred and secular, then it does not make sense for public professionals to operate without any knowledge of how these activities fit into religious life. Courses on religion should be offered in nonprofit management programs, and workshops must be developed for current social welfare and development professionals.

3. Leaders in denominations and congregations must learn the basic contours of local government, both city and neighborhood, and of the social service community. Seminaries should offer courses on social service, and development organizations and workshops must be arranged for current religious professionals. In truth, such a requirement runs counter to the inclination of most seminarians much more than courses on religious organizations would for aspiring civil servants. But the information must be made available; if seminarians choose not to fill such classes, perhaps that will be a useful clue about the likelihood of successful partnerships.

4. Information gatekeepers should be identified and nurtured in every urban neighborhood. This relatively small group of professionals, drawn from both the secular and religious communities, must be conversant with the baseline data about their respective neighborhoods. Toward that end, they must be in regular contact with the data managers who maintain and analyze that data. The gatekeepers must keep regular contact with city hall, local foundations, local service agencies, and local religious groups. Their job would not be to administrate local activities or to regulate the flow of funds. They would exist to keep all local organizations informed about what is going on in their own neighborhood or at the metropolitan level.

No matter what precautions are built in, there is always some risk that information gatekeepers will choose to direct information to some leaders or organizations and not to others in accordance with their own personal agendas. Moreover, turnover among information gatekeepers could be problematic even with overlap and redundancy built into neighborhood leadership. But those risks, bad as they might be, are preferable to the selective, idiosyncratic ways that information is currently distributed. In a system of overlapping information gatekeepers, every organization and every leader would have a point of reference. In the current system of information delivery, every person or organization must recreate the process each time new information is needed or else, as is more likely, those who can afford the time and network building to acquire information will thrive, while those who cannot will not. (A subset of this affordability is information technology. Although it is tempting to think that this information could be relayed via the internet, thus eliminating the need for gatekeepers as middlemen, this is not a plausible strategy for congregations and small nonprofits in the near future.)

In this new, mixed environment for services and development, the potential for problems is real. Government may get involved with religion in ways that challenge our understanding of the Constitution. Congregations may find their other ministries compromised by secular goals and rules. Certain individuals may gain too much power if they are singled out for training as the consulting gatekeepers.

These problems are real, but the alternatives are worse. On the one hand, we could seek to establish clear, rigid boundaries for government, private service organizations, and the faith community. Such boundaries have never existed, however, and all of the movement of the past two decades has been in the direction of greater, not smaller overlap.

On the other hand, we might continue the haphazard, uneven process of sharing information and ad hoc partnerships that we are experimenting with today. We should be prepared, however, for the "winners" in such an arrangement to be those who can best afford information and can most easily build coalitions rather than those who might best be able to provide the needed assistance.

Given those alternatives, we must choose to face squarely the fact of a public and private, sacred and secular mix whether it makes us uncomfortable or not. We must allow organizations to make their own choices about where and how much and in what way they will participate. But we must also help them make the best possible choices by ensuring that the information necessary for an informed decision is available.

Working through the new partnerships in the interest of generating social capital will be painful for every city. Cities can ease that pain, however, if local governments and foundations insist on a broadly accessible pool of baseline data, encourage and reward cross-functional training for public and religious leaders, and nurture information gatekeepers who serve as consultants for specific neighborhoods.

This book has consistently argued that assumptions concerning congregations must always be checked against the best available data and that expectations regarding congregations must be lowered. The first half of that task is made more difficult by the fact that good data is rare in most places. But the argument is not, nor could it ever be, that attempts to work with congregations in order to build better communities and provide better social services should be abandoned. Congregations want to help and they can.

Once everyone has a clearer view of what congregations want to do and what their real capacity is, then they can begin the hard work of forging partnerships that benefit from the strengths—and avoid the weaknesses—of each of the partners. But this work will not begin until those in the civic world know more about religion, those in the religious sphere know more about government and nonprofit organizations, and general information about available programs and funding opportunities is more widely available.

These goals will not be accomplished until seminaries prepare pastors and staff people for urban ministry by teaching them how the urban context operates. They will not be accomplished until schools of public policy teach about religious organizations. This has nothing to do with teaching theology or doctrine, but rather with emphasizing how different polities operate and the role different kinds of religious organizations play in their respective communities. Finally, it will not happen until government and foundation leaders make the commitment to include religious organizations as full and equal partners in the exchange of program information.

# 9  Realistic Expectations

> . . . people are drawn to religious organizations primarily because of the ways those organizations can meet their personal needs; but many of those needs center on the desire to strengthen and transmit—to family and others—moral values, both in word and deed. . . . The majority of people continue to expect religion, and especially religious organizations, to contribute to the public good: first, by providing a moral underpinning for individuals in both public and private life, by upholding moral ideals in the public realm; and second, by providing specific practical, charitable, and philanthropic service. (Jeavons 1994)

Some supporters of faith-based reforms are fond of saying that partnership between government and the religious community is not new. They point out correctly that groups like Catholic Charities and the Jewish Federation have received public funding in various forms for decades.

The point is well taken as far as it goes. There is nothing new about the principle of public-private partnership, including partnership with groups who have religious affiliation. But it is somewhat disingenuous to press the point too hard. Most public partnership with religious organizations has been conducted at a fairly high level of abstraction. Government contracted with a number of large charitable organizations, some of which had religious roots. All of the contracting organizations—secular or sacred—were subject to the same federal guidelines prohibiting hiring discrimination or evangelizing.

Religious organizations dealt with this by forming separate nonprofit corporations that handled their charitable activities and dealt with government funds. The groups were religious, to be sure, but they were generally nonsectarian. The best analogy might be with hospitals. Some hospitals, we all know, have religious roots and continuing religious affiliations. But we expect all hospitals to offer the same standard of medical care, and most of us would choose the one with the best expertise to meet our current needs. None of us would be surprised to find that any hospital—with or without religious roots—was eligible for government funding for research or administration. Put simply, the religious affiliation may be important, but the organizations are known to be nonsectarian.

In many ways, social service agencies with religious roots have operated much the same. Some, like Goodwill, came to be seen as not especially religious at all. Others, like Jewish Federation or Catholic Charities or Lutheran Child and Family Services, were acknowledged to have special expertise with certain groups. For instance, when Russian Jewish immigrants come to Indianapolis, it is widely expected that the Jewish Federation will provide the base for their service support. Why would they not? And if the same government funding that might have gone through a secular organization to provide these services can be channeled through a Jewish organization to provide them better, who would complain?

But the changes embodied in Secretary Cisneros's push for local, neighborhood involvement by faith-based groups were enormous. The development of an Office for Faith-based Initiatives at HUD and the passage of the so-called Charitable Choice clause of the 1996 Personal Responsibility and Work Opportunity Reconciliation Act showed the shift's true significance. Government had moved beyond partnership at the high level of charitable organizations and was looking to small, faith-based groups, especially congregations, to become neighborhood-based social service organizations. Some restrictions, such as those on hiring discrimination and displaying religious symbols, were removed to make it easier for congregations to serve in these roles, though they were still prohibited from directly evangelizing.

As this book has made clear, the 2001 Bush administration did not invent the concept of local faith-based services based in congregations; it just attempted to push the existing logic out into a wider sphere of government activity. Many political conservatives were already predisposed to like the combination of smaller government and smaller bureaucracy, coupled with religious values and local control. They truly wanted social services—welfare—delivered by local groups capable of treating the recipients as individuals with moral and spiritual as well as material needs. Government continues to contract with the large service organizations that have religious roots. But the emphasis, the hope, and the expectation have shifted to local religious organizations, especially congregations.

Given this shift in emphasis, it is not surprising that civil libertarians and other constitutional critics have stepped forward (Kramnick and Moore 1997). They are unlikely to be placated by claims that "government has contracted with faith-based groups for years" because they can clearly see the change. Few have any quarrel with funding service agencies with either sacred or secular roots, so long as standard federal guidelines apply. But the claim of welfare reformers is that limitations on displaying religious objects, reading religious texts, or hiring only fellow adherents of one's faith restrict local religious groups unfairly. Faith-based reformers believe they are leveling the playing field. Civil libertarian critics believe they are crossing the line separating church and state.

Not surprisingly, then, much of the early debate about Charitable Choice and related welfare reforms has focused on questions of church and state. There is strong, often emotional disagreement about the appropriate amount of religious activity that can exist in any program that receives public funding. This book has intentionally avoided most of that debate because legal and constitutional experts, as well as politicians, are in a much better position to conduct it.

But it is imperative to note that discussion about faith-based reforms must be conducted on other levels as well. There is a disturbing tendency in arguments about the legal ramifications for church and state for each side to grant, even to assume, that faith-based providers are naturally preferable. That congregations would be able to provide these services and that they should want to do so seems to be taken on faith, so to speak. But it makes no sense to spend months, possibly even years, battling over the constitutionality of plans that may simply be impractical. The question is not only whether congregations and other faith-based groups ought, legally, to be eligible for public support but also whether they would be able to meet the expectations set for them even if they did receive it (Farnsley 1998, 2000a).

The short answer to that question is that some congregations would do quite well with public funding, improving on the excellent mission programs they already support. Some other congregations would be drawn into social services and would also be good providers. Those who advocate faith-based welfare reform, those who believe that inner-city congregations are the last, best hope for distressed neighborhoods, can justifiably point to examples of good faith-based programs and can outline their plans to develop many more.

The assumptions that drive faith-based reforms are not themselves without merit. Some congregations truly are local organizations, either drawing their members from the area surrounding their houses of worship or developing one or more sets of special bonds with those neighbors. In many urban neighborhoods, congregations are the strongest—if not the only—local institutions. Similarly, congregations have relatively little overhead, and some, at least, are unconstrained by layers of bureaucracy. Finally, there can be little doubt that congregations are in the business of treating the whole person, of imparting beliefs and values as well as hot meals and winter clothing.

As should be clear by now, the point of this book has not been to belittle congregations or to criticize the many benefits they provide the rest of society. Some congregations are large organizations with substantial resources, including the ability to spend their own money on social services and to conduct the administration necessary both to receive and to expend public funds effectively. Some of these have strong ties to the community they would serve and are able to emphasize the importance of character and values without crossing the line into outright evangelism or proselytization. The point of this book is to dampen some of the hottest enthusiasm about the capacity of most congregations to meet pressing social needs. Most congregations are relatively small organizations with limited resources. They exist to provide opportunities for worship and character development for members and their children. They are not tightly tied to the neighborhood where their facilities lie, nor do most of the members live there. They have little or no experience writing grants or administering programs. And their strongest outreach programs are direct evangelism in which they challenge others to understand and accept their beliefs.

## Where Do We Go from Here?

How, then, do we best assess the related facts that some congregations are capable of providing the advantages that faith-based reformers expect of them but that most are not? How can we use this information to monitor the progress of faith-based reforms, recognizing that some such reforms are inevitable whatever judicial decisions come to inform the process of government funding? As should be clear, the first thing we can do is to lower our expectations and see congregations for what they are. We can try to understand that their mission activities grow out of their theological commitments grounded in worship and character development, but that missions are not the defining ends in and of themselves. Beyond this, we can look at practical steps that will create a stronger network among the many organizations, both religious and secular, that make up the entire ecology in which communities are developed and services are delivered.

## Professional Training

One excellent place to start would be in the training of professionals to staff these community organizations. At present, schools of social work or of public affairs do a very poor job of teaching students about religious organizations. This is partly because local religion has been seen, mistakenly, as a kind of voluntary parallel to the true professionals in secular social work or in civic administration. Social service professionals in the Salvation Army or Catholic Charities were regarded as colleagues, but pastors and community ministers were regarded as outsiders. In a society of faith-based reform, such attitudes will have to change.

Another reason these schools have done a poor job of preparing students for the new environment is that religion is still too often seen as a system of ideas and beliefs. For future leaders in civil society, the defining aspect of religious groups should be their styles of *organization*. Admittedly, the organization follows from the beliefs, but this is less crucial as a practical matter. Until leaders in the nonprofit world and in government come to grips with differences in polity and in pastoral leadership, they will be ineffective at working with potential faith-based partners.

Seminaries do a similarly poor job, if not worse. Teachers of social work and public policy may not recognize religion's role in the community ecology, but teachers of ministry have no excuse for underestimating the importance of local government and social work. They are right to continue to emphasize preaching, teaching, and counseling, because that is what congregational members—the employers, in this case—will most expect from new pastors. But seminaries must prepare their students for the expectation that their congregations will be service organizations. And insofar as those congregations will want to perform effective missions, as most surely will, then the pastors should be prepared to understand that they, too, are part of a community's ecology. They need not learn how to become more like secular social service groups or like government, but they must learn to understand and articulate the differences between their organizations and others in the ecology as well as to identify points of overlap.

Specialization, including the differentiation of organizational types, is crucial to the development of any ecology, and this is no naïve argument that everyone must work to downplay the differences or even to promote the overlap. But the fact remains that there *is* overlap, especially in the areas of community development and social service. There is no clean division of labor among government, secular nonprofit groups, and religious groups. Whether these groups cooperate and form fruitful partnerships or see themselves as competitors, their interplay will be strengthened and sharpened when each group better understands the other's function and the organizational style that supports it. Anyone who is serious about faith-based reform must advocate the enrichment of professional training for leadership in any of these areas to include basic information about the others.

## Information Gatekeepers

Another crucial step in building effective partnerships within the bounds of realistic expectations would be to establish the sort of free flow of information advocated throughout this book and elucidated in Chapter 8. Some person or people, located in some organization within each community, must take responsibility for bridging the gaps that keep information from moving equally to government employees, nonprofit workers, volunteers, and faith-based groups. Moreover, these gatekeepers must somehow be connected to one another so that information moves equitably not only among organizations within a neighborhood but also between and among the different neighborhoods that normally have very unequal access to resources.

Even if such a person or group existed, and even if they were themselves "networked," a variety of communication problems remain. Many faith-based groups do not have a staff member, volunteer, or even a committee whose responsibility it is to gather and process community-based information. As is by now clear, few congregations can afford to hire a community minister. Congregational members are famous for providing volunteer hours and serving on committees, but so much internal work is needed to keep congregations going as worship communities that it is not always easy to identify the person responsible for missions, much less the one responsible specifically for local missions.

Obviously each congregation must work out for itself who might serve in this role and how it would be approached relative to the many other tasks within the group. Nonetheless, this is unlikely to happen until it is clear that useful information is available and that taking advantage of it might enhance the congregation's ministries. Congregations are notorious for giving sacrificially and for not always asking, "What's in it for me?" But in a world of finite time and resources, the advantages of participation in a functioning network of ideas and information must be made clear.

It is difficult to say, therefore, who bears responsibility for trying to assemble an information network composed of trusted gatekeepers in viable organizations. There are obvious difficulties in having any one religious group start it, because their efforts could be seen as self-serving by other religious groups and could well be ignored by local government or the professional social work community. In cities where one religious group is dominant—say, Catholics in Providence, or Latter Day Saints in Salt Lake City—then their group must form key components of any such network.

In other cities, though, local government or local foundations must take the lead, trying hard to reach out across theological divides. This seems to have been the philosophy underlying Stephen Goldsmith's Front Porch Alliance. However, the FPA seemed at times to work so directly with congregations that it bypassed the traditional community organizations such as Community Centers of Indianapolis. Long-term success depends on building better ties among such groups.

It is, of course, easy to sit in front of a keyboard and say that communication is crucial and that more effort must be expended on network building, when the people in the trenches are overloaded just trying to meet each day's needs. But someone or some organization must step outside the day-to-day crisis mode and say that the commitment to a better exchange of information and ideas is worth the immediate cost.

## Forthright Evaluation

One final way to strengthen the entire ecology of community organizations and to make faith-based groups more effective partners is to be more forthright about resources and about untapped potential. This could be best accomplished through controlled evaluation procedures.

From the time faith-based reforms hit the national news, scholars have been reminding anyone who will listen that very little data exists on the subject. Proponents believe that faith-based reforms will improve the lives of those served. Even critics tend to focus on legal issues rather than on actual performance. Critical, straightforward evaluation of faith-based programs is the best way to approach the problem. But that work cannot be left to university researchers. It requires the commitment of all of those engaged in community building or social service delivery.

Anyone who has ever worked in those fields knows already the problem with evaluation. Virtually everyone involved has a vested interest. The point is not that faith-based or secular service groups will be intentionally dishonest, but they are often inclined to put their activities in the best possible light. In the worst case, they cloak poor performance in righteous language: "Maybe we didn't help as many as we would have liked, but if one heart is changed, isn't that what it is all about?"

In a stable environment, the sponsors of programs bear responsibility for the evaluation. Even if those who run the programs hope to put the best possible spin on their efforts, those who provide the money have an obligation to cut through that and decide for themselves. However, in an era of politically charged reforms, those sponsors have a vested interest as well. Mayor Goldsmith wanted and needed the Front Porch Alliance to work, not least because he planned to use this model as an advisor to George W. Bush. CHIP wants the congregations-as-partners initiative to succeed not only because it wants to serve the homeless population better but also to show the Lilly Endowment that such efforts succeed. For their own part, the Lilly Endowment is always interested in activities that enhance the ministries of congregations and promote their standing in the community. In Juvenile Court, Judge Payne wanted to prove that faith-based counselors adding moral and spiritual values were better able to help young offenders.

So who checks on these groups and evaluates their efforts impartially? Others in the social service network may criticize, but they are also subject to the charge of self interest. After all, if faith-based groups do the job better for less money, where does that leave social work professionals? Academic researchers like myself can evaluate, though we are also subject to the criticism that we have an interest in perpetuating some institutions over others or that we have inherent ideological biases.

Over time, the ultimate judge of these reforms will be the public, at least insofar as tax expenditures are concerned. What the Lilly Endowment chooses to do with its money is its own business, but the tax-paying public and all of those who contribute to groups like the United Way have a right and responsibility to think these issues through. But they will have trouble getting good comparative information unless they demand it, because so many participants have an interest in presenting the facts in ways that suit their purposes.

The best we can hope for is an honest, open appraisal of the magnitude of our social problems and the resources available to address them. I have attempted to begin that conversation here by shedding light on some of the assumptions about congregations as faith-based providers. But the same could be done for other organizations within the ecology of community organizations. And as faith-based reforms go forward, more evidence will emerge that must be consistently evaluated and compared to other methods of service delivery or community building.

## What Congregations Do

Even as we constantly compare and evaluate, though, it is important that we not lose sight of the many benefits congregations offer civil society beyond the provision of services. There is good reason to believe that congregations make their largest contribution to the community by shaping virtuous people who will go out into the world as our fellow citizens. Most congregations have just such an image of themselves. They do mission work because they are called to do it, but they are called to it as a *worshipping community.* Mission may, in some cases, be their most driving ambition, their community's foremost goal. But it is not their reason for being.

Some congregations see participation in civic life as a logical extension of their other missions. Others see a separation between the civic participation of individuals and their calling as a group. They envision their congregation as holy and separate, a spiritual haven from the secular realm. They work very intentionally to keep it free from direct involvement in worldly affairs. A prominent Republican Party committeeman made the point to us clearly that his church "plays no role in the infrastructure of society." Yet "involvement in community is not hypocrisy for the church members," he said. "Church members are welcomed, even encouraged, to be involved in civil society. But the 'church collective' cannot do so because it is not founded in the scriptures."

Even congregations that see no theological limitations on civic participation by the group as an organization resist the characterization of their congregation as a social service group because that is just not how they ordinarily think of it. Their church or synagogue may practice many social ministries and gladly engage the outside world, but they still picture themselves fundamentally as a community of worship. They meet together for services and teach religious education classes to develop as people trying to improve their relationship to God. They choose their clergy and manage their time toward that end. Even the call to serve others through well-organized programs is seen primarily as an outgrowth of spiritual development.

A different survey conducted as part of our research supports that view. There we found a direct link between congregational involvement and what most people would call good citizenship. In a survey of 600 residents of inner-city Indianapolis neighborhoods, we found some interesting linkages among factors such as worship attendance, neighborhood involvement, and civic participation (Wright and Farnsley 1997).

The short version of those findings is that more frequent attendance at worship is associated with stronger feelings of community, more familiarity with one's neighbors, more frequent contact with political officials, and a greater likelihood of belonging to secular civic organizations. It is, of course, possible that some people are just "joiners." The sort of person who is likely to be involved in a congregation is also likely to be involved in other groups. One reason people attend worship is that they enjoy the sense of community, and these same people may have a stronger, more active and involved sense of experiencing community in other venues as well.

But we found that the relationships overlap and grow stronger as each layer is added. People have a slightly stronger sense of community, know more of their neighbors, and are more likely to be politically active—say, to write a letter to the city council or to join civic organizations—if the congregation where they worship is also located in the neighborhood where they live. To the degree that religious involvement and neighborhood life overlap, they are mutually reinforcing. The relationships are stronger still if one's circle of friends and neighbors overlaps with that congregational involvement. Someone whose fellow worshippers are also part of her circle of friends is more likely to feel embedded in a community and more likely to be politically active or to join civic groups than someone without that overlap. And if those fellow worshippers and that circle of friends are also neighbors in the geographic sense of the term, then the likelihood of civic and political engagement and of a strong sense of community is even further increased.

These survey results underlined what our common sense already told us. There is a mutually reinforcing relationship between worship, local community ties, a sense of political efficacy, and broader civic participation. There is good reason to believe that congregational membership and worship attendance contribute not only to the sense of internal community experienced by those within a congregation but also to a stronger sense of community in general and to a greater likelihood of civic involvement. In short, religion has a positive effect on what most of us would call "good citizenship," and that effect grows stronger the more local and personal it is.

The new emphasis on congregations as organizations, as builders of social capital, and as soldiers in what President Bush has called "the Armies of Compassion," contains considerable risk for congregations. It would be very easy for some of them to begin to see themselves as nonprofit service organizations, especially when more than two-thirds of those *outside* of congregations see them in that light.

Those of us who study congregations as organizations must be especially careful not to contribute to that misunderstanding of what is essential to most congregations' activities. Whatever external missions they do or do not support, congregations play a valuable role as mediating institutions by helping to create good citizens embedded in supportive communities. And they do this, not by intending to, but simply by *being* communities of faith. It is hard to imagine what other institution might play that role as well as they do.

By no means does this lead to the conclusion that congregations should "only" take care of their own members and should stop acting as social organizations to change the world outside their doors. There is much that congregations can do if they choose, both on their own and in concert with their denominations or other special purpose groups.

But congregations need not apologize for specializing in moral formation and the creation of communities of worship. For one thing, it is not clear that congregations *owe* the wider society anything. Most choose to contribute sacrificially as part of their calling, but in the larger social calculus, surely everyone agrees that congregations give more than they take. More importantly, though, there are good reasons to believe that congregations benefit society precisely by being communities of worship engaged in moral formation.

The rest of us should keep in mind that congregations are not only—and maybe not even best—defined by their external activities as organizations. They are about the creation of community, and that community, however fragile it seems at times, is no small matter in a society where the most powerful institutions elevate the status of the individual.

Congregations contribute to a healthy society when they function as local communities—whether defined geographically or socially—capable of producing citizens who are secure in their social relationships, prepared to act politically, and willing to shoulder their share or more of civic responsibility. Their social service activities are a beneficial by-product, but to define them as service organizations is to lose sight of the benefits to society inherent in congregations doing well what they do best.

# Bibliography

Ammerman, Nancy. 1996. "Bowling Together: Congregations and the American Civic Order." University Lecture in Religion, Arizona State University.

———. 2001. "Doing Good in American Communities: Congregations and Service Organizations Working Together." Preliminary research report of the Hartford Institute for Religion Research.

Ammerman, Nancy, with Arthur Farnsley et al. 1997. *Congregation and Community.* New Brunswick, N.J.: Rutgers University Press.

Bartkowski, John, Helen Regis, Neil White, and Melinda Chow. 1999. "Can Religious Congregations Satisfy Those Who Hunger and Thirst for Justice?" Research Report of the Southern Regional Development Center.

Beliefnet.com. 2001. Interview with Rev. Jerry Falwell, March 6.

Benjamin, Ellen. 1997. "Philanthropic Institutions and the Small Religious Nonprofit." *Nonprofit and Voluntary Sector Quarterly* 26 (suppl.): 529–43.

Berger, Peter, and R. J. Neuhaus. 1977. *To Empower People: The Role of Mediating Structures in Public Policy.* Washington, D.C.: American Enterprise Institute.

Bodenhamer, David, and Robert Barrows. 1994. *Encyclopedia of Indianapolis.* Bloomington: Indiana University Press.

Boris, Elizabeth, and Tobi Jennifer Printz. 1997. "Report on Services and Capacity of Religious Congregations in the Washington, D.C., Metropolitan Area." Research report of the Center on Nonprofits and Philanthropy, Urban Institute.

Boris, Elizabeth, and Eugene Steuerle. 1999. "What Charities Cannot Do." Urban Institute Report, October 1.

Bos, David. 1993. *A Practical Guide to Community Ministry.* Louisville, Ky.: Westminster/ John Knox Press.

Bradley, Martin, Norman Green, Dale Jones, Mac Lynn, and Lou McNeil. 1992. *Churches and Church Membership in the United States.* Atlanta, Ga.: Glenmary Research Center.

Bush, George W. 2001. "Rallying the Armies of American Compassion." Presidential Directive.

Byrd, Michael. 1997. "Determining Frames of Reference for Religiously Based Organizations: A Case of Neo-Alinsky Efforts to Mobilize Congregational Resources." *Nonprofit and Voluntary Sector Quarterly* 26 (suppl.): 122–38.

Carlson-Theis, Stanley. 2000. "Charitable Choice for Welfare and Community Services: An Implementation Guide for State, Local, and Federal Officials." Handbook from Center for Public Justice.

Casanova, Jose. 1994. *Public Religions in the Modern World.* Chicago: University of Chicago Press.

Chaves, Mark. 1998. "Religious Congregations and Welfare Reform: Who Will Take Advantage of 'Charitable Choice'?" Working Paper Series, Nonprofit Sector Research Fund, the Aspen Institute.

———. 2001. "Religious Congregations and Welfare Reform." *Society* 38, no. 2: 21–27.

Chaves, Mark, and Lynn Higgins. 1992. "Comparing the Community Involvement of

Black and White Congregations." *Journal for the Scientific Study of Religion* 31: 425–40.

Chaves, Mark, and William Tsitsos. 2001. "Congregations and Social Services: What They Do, How They Do It, and with Whom." Working paper of the Nonprofit Sector Research.

Cisneros, Henry. 1996. "Higher Ground: Faith Communities and Community Building." Essay published as a brochure by Department of Housing and Urban Development.

Cnaan, Ram. 1997. "Social and Community Involvement of Religious Congregations Housed in Historic Religious Properties: Findings from a Six-city Study." Final report to Partners for Sacred Places.

Cnaan, Ram, with Robert Wineburg and Stephanie Boddie. 2000. *The Newer Deal: Social Work and Religion in Partnership.* New York: Columbia University Press.

Demerath, N. J., Peter Dobkin Hall, Terry Schmitt, and Rhys Williams, eds. 1997. *Sacred Companies: Organizational Aspects of Religion and Religious Aspects of Organizations.* New York: Oxford University Press.

Diamond, Etan. 1997. "Wandering in the Wilderness: Religious Mobility in the Modern Metropolis." Paper presented to the Organization of American Historians.

Dimaggio, Paul, and Walter Powell. 1988. "The Iron Cage Revisited: Institutional Isomorphism and Collective Rationality in Organizational Fields." In *Community Organizations,* edited by Carl Milofsky. New Haven, Conn.: Yale University Press.

DiIulio, John. 1997a. "Lord's Work: Church and the 'Civil Society Sector.'" Research report to the Brookings Institution.

———. 1997b. "Spiritual Capital Can Save Inner-City Youth." Research report to the Brookings Institution.

———. 1999. "Supporting Black Churches: Faith, Outreach, and the Inner-City Poor." Research report to the Brookings Institution.

Dionne, E. J., and John DiIulio. 1999. "What's God Got to Do with the American Experiment?" Brookings Institution, *Brookings Review* (Spring): 4–8.

Eiesland, Nancy L. 2000. *A Particular Place: Urban Restructuring and Religious Ecology in a Southern Exurb.* New Brunswick, N.J.: Rutgers University Press.

Etindi, Diana. 1998. "Charitable Choice and its Implications for Faith-Based Organizations." An occasional paper of the Hudson Institute, August.

Farnsley, Arthur. 1998. "Churches to the Rescue?" *Christian Century,* December 9, 1182–84.

———. 2000a. "Ten Good Questions about Faith-Based Partnerships and Welfare Reform." Booklet published by the Polis Center.

———. 2000b. "Congregations, Local Knowledge, and Devolution." *Review of Religious Research* 42, no. 1: 97–111. (Cited at length by permission of the Religious Research Association.)

———. 2001a. "Can Faith-Based Organizations Compete?" *Nonprofit and Voluntary Sector Quarterly* 30, no. 1 (March): 99–111. (Portions reproduced by permission of Sage Publishing.)

———. 2001b. "Faith-Based Action: Who Benefits?" *Christian Century,* March 14, 12–15.

Franklin, Robert. 1997. *Another Day's Journey: Black Churches Confronting the American Crisis.* Minneapolis: Fortress Press.

Gibson, James G., Thomas Kingsley, and Joseph B. McNeely. 1997. *Community Building Comes of Age.* Report to the Urban Institute, May.

Goldsmith, Stephen. 1998. Speech to Columbia Law School, March 12.

Green, Clifford. 1996. *Churches, Cities, and Human Community: Urban Ministry in the United States 1945–1985.* Grand Rapids, Mich.: Eerdmans.

Hall, Peter. 1997. "Apples and Oranges: Definitional Dilemmas in Assessing the Place of Religion in the Organizational Universe." Presentation to Independent Sector research forum, Alexandria, Va., March.

Jackson, Maxie, John Schweitzer, Marvin Cato, and Reynard Blake. 1997. "Faith-Based Institutions' Community and Economic Development Programs Serving Black Communities in Michigan." Research report of the Community Foundation for Southeastern Michigan.

Jeavons, Thomas. 1994. *When the Bottom Line Is Faithfulness: The Management of Christian Service Organizations.* Bloomington: Indiana University Press.

Jeavons, Thomas, and Ram Cnaan. 1997. "The Formation, Transitions, and Evolution of Small Religious Organizations." *Nonprofit and Voluntary Sector Quarterly* 26 (suppl.): 62–84.

Klein, Joe. 1997. "In God They Trust." *New Yorker Magazine,* June 16, 40–48.

Koch, Jerome, and D. Paul Johnson. 1997. "The Ecumenical Outreach Coalition: A Case Study of Converging Interests and Network Formation for Church and Community Cooperation." *Nonprofit and Voluntary Sector Quarterly* 26, no. 3: 343–58.

Kramnick, Isaac, and Laurence Moore. 1997. "Can the Churches Save the Cities? Faith-Based Services and the Constitution." *American Prospect,* no. 35: 47–53.

Lenkowsky, Leslie. 2001. "Funding the Faithful: Why Bush Is Right." *Commentary* 11 (June): 19–25.

Lincoln, C. Eric, and Lawrence Mamiya. 1990. *The Black Church in the African-American Experience.* Durham, N.C.: Duke University Press.

Lilly Endowment. 1994. "Religious Institutions as Partners in Community-Based Development." Rainbow Research Group report.

Linnan, John. 1995. "Re-thinking the Urban Parish." Unpublished paper.

Livezey, Lowell. 2000. *Public Religion and Urban Transformation.* New York: New York University Press.

McGreevey, John. 1996. *Parish Boundaries: The Catholic Encounter with Race in the Twentieth-Century Urban North.* Chicago: University of Chicago Press.

McKnight, John, and John Kretzmann. 1993. *Building Communities from the Inside Out: A Path Toward Finding and Mobilizing Community Assets.* Evanston, Ill.: Northwestern University Press.

Messer, John. 1998. "Agency, Communion, and the Formation of Social Capital." *Nonprofit and Voluntary Sector Quarterly* 27, no. 1: 5–12.

Milbank, Dana. 1997. "In God They Trust: Michigan Now Relies on Churches to Help People Leave Welfare." *Wall Street Journal,* March 17, 1.

Milofsky, Carl. 1988. "Scarcity and Community: A Resource Allocation Theory of Community and Mass Society Organizations." In *Community Organizations,* edited by Carl Milofsky. New Haven, Conn.: Yale University Press.

———. 1997. "Organization from Community: A Case Study of Congregational Renewal." *Nonprofit and Voluntary Sector Quarterly* 26 (suppl.): 139–60.

Olasky, Marvin. 1992. *The Tragedy of American Compassion.* Washington, D.C., and Lanham, Md.: Regnery Gateway Press.

Orr, John. 2000. "Faith Based Organizations and Welfare Reform: California Religious Community Capacity Study Qualitative Findings and Conclusions." Research report of the Center for Religion and Civic Culture, University of Southern California, November.

Orr, John, Donald Miller, Wade Clark Roof, and J. Gordon Melton. 1994. "Politics of the Spirit: Religion and Multiethnicity in Los Angeles." Research report, University of Southern California.

Printz, Tobi Jennifer. 1998. "Faith Based Service Providers in the Nation's Capital: Can They Do More?" Urban Institute, Charting Civil Society Project, April.

Putnam, Robert. 1995a. "Bowling Alone: America's Declining Social Capital." *Journal of Democracy* 6: 65–78.

———. 1995b. "Tuning In, Tuning Out: The Strange Disappearance of Social Capital in America." Ithiel de Sola Pool Lecture. Reprinted in *Political Science and Politics*, 28, no. 4: 664–84.

———. 2001. *Bowling Alone: The Collapse and Revival of American Community.* New York: Touchstone Books.

Queen, Edward, ed. 2000. *Serving Those in Need: A Handbook for Managing Faith-Based Human Services Organizations.* San Francisco: Jossey-Bass Publishing.

Ramsay, Meredith. 1998. "Redeeming the City: Exploring the Relationship between Church and Metropolis." *Urban Affairs Review* 33, no. 5: 595–626.

Shapiro, Joseph. 1996. "Can Churches Save America?" *U.S. News and World Report*, September 9, 46–53.

Sherman, Amy. 1995. "Cross Purposes: Will Conservative Welfare Reform Corrupt Religious Charities?" A research report of the Heritage Foundation.

———. 2000. "A Survey of Church-Government Anti-poverty Partnerships." A research report of the Hudson Institute.

———. 2001. *Charitable Choice Handbook for Ministry Leaders.* Washington, D.C.: Center for Public Justice.

Stone, Melissa, and Miriam Wood. 1997. "Governance and the Small, Religiously Affiliated Social Service Provider." *Nonprofit and Voluntary Sector Quarterly* 26 (suppl.): 44–61.

Trulear, Harold Dean. 2000. "Faith Based Institutions and High Risk Youth." Report of Public/Private Ventures, Spring.

Wallis, Jim. 1997. "With Unconditional Love: An Interview with John DiIulio." *Sojourners*, October.

Warner, R. Stephen. 1994. "The Place of the Congregation in the Contemporary Religious Context." In *American Congregations*, edited by James Wind and James Lewis. Chicago: University of Chicago Press.

Wind, James P., and James W. Lewis. 1994. *American Congregations.* Vol. 2, *New Perspectives in the Study of Congregations.* Chicago: University of Chicago Press.

Wineburg, Robert. 2000. *A Limited Partnership: The Politics of Religion, Welfare, and Social Service.* New York: Columbia University Press.

Wolpert, Julian. 1997. "The Role of Small Religious Nonprofits in Changing Urban Neighborhoods." *Nonprofit and Voluntary Sector Quarterly* 26 (suppl.): 14–28.

Woodson, Robert. 1998. *The Triumphs of Joseph: How Today's Community Healers Are Reviving Our Streets and Neighborhoods.* New York: Free Press.

Wright, Eric, and Arthur Farnsley. 1997. Neighborhood survey of 600 neighborhood residents conducted by the Polis Center, Indianapolis, Ind.

# Index

Arthur E. Farnsley II is Senior Research Associate at The Polis Center, an urban think tank. His commentary on religion, politics, and public life has appeared in magazines and on the op-ed pages of newspapers across the country, as well as in academic journals and in the book *Southern Baptist Politics* (1994). During the late 1990s, he consulted on Indianapolis's most prominent experiments in faith-based social service partnerships. He is currently a member of The Rockefeller Institute of Government's Roundtable on Religion and Social Welfare Policy.